Author's Note

This image honors my four sisters: Margaret (90, top left), Annette (76, top right), Helen (91, bottom left), and Virginia (89, bottom right). They have played an important role in developing my sensitivity to older women and to learning about this life stage throughout my life. I thank them for their contributions.

(Painting courtesy of our dear friend and fine artist James Fiorentino.)

EMERGING FROM THE SHADOWS

*The Needs of Older Women
and the Benefits of Supporting Them*

Dr. Ron Hofsess

&

Dr. Christy Hofsess, Editor

*A publication in association with
the Trust in the Lives
of Older Women Program*

Llumina
Press

ISBN: 978-1-62550-124-0

Printed in the United States of America by Llumina Press

Library of Congress Control Number: 2014933908

*This book is dedicated to all
older women in the world.*

♀ CONTENTS ♙♙

♙♙♙ ♙♙♙ ♙♙♙ ♙♙♙ ♀ ♙♙♙ ♙♙♙ ♙♙♙ ♙♙♙

Chapter 4: The Voices of Older Women and Supporters

Chapter 5: Envisioning the Future

Chapter 6: Reflections and Responses

PREFACE

The idea for the development of support groups geared toward older women (i.e., Trust in the Lives of Older Women) emerged long before I intentionally started creating them. This passion has its underpinnings in my childhood and was influenced by my family and community. Like many who discover and live out their life's passion, I used my early life experiences as the underlying foundation of my work.

I am the youngest of 12 children. I have seven brothers and four sisters. I was an uncle as soon as I was born; two of my sisters each had one child before my mother gave birth to me. My three oldest siblings are women, and each could have easily been my mother. In fact, all three were surrogate mothers at times. My mother could have easily been my grandmother; she was 42 when she gave birth to me.

As a result of my family experience and sibling position, I was introduced at a young age to a community of older women—mainly through my mother's connections. She would often host the "Priscilla Circle," a term for her women friends from the local Methodist Church. The women who came to our house for meetings ranged in age from their late forties to well into their eighties and nineties. As a group and individually, these women engaged me personally and were very kind to me. My mother also belonged to the local garden club and would often have her older women friends to our house as well. In addition, our weekly trips to church gave me regular exposure to older women. On Sunday mornings, we would head for church early so that my dad could make two or three stops to pick up my mother's friends. As such, I became comfortable and interested in relating to older women. They were a regular part of my life.

My sisters often reminded me of the importance of being sensitive to women—and today, especially to older women. For example, my sisters have sent newspaper clippings that describe issues and experiences older women are dealing with in their lives. They have also tended to call and tell me about television shows related to the issues facing older women. My sisters have always been very supportive of my research interest and have helped keep me tuned in to the needs of older women.

My interest in "trust" (see Chapter 3) evolved from my family system. I was given a great deal of freedom early in my youth. Given the size of the family, my parents trusted my siblings and me with the judgment to make good decisions. This freedom allowed me to make my own choices at an early age. I wasn't given any curfews, so I determined how to best use my discretionary time. I had a job, bought my own clothes, and behaved responsibly. As a result, I learned to trust myself and to discern trustworthiness in others. Little did I know that these early family and community experiences would lead me down a path I am extremely passionate about today: creating Trust in the Lives of Older Women (TLOW) groups (see Chapter 3).

My academic and life work experience in human services furthered my professional focus and provided me with a foundation of skills and knowledge from which I was able to bring my passion into professional action. I have a B.A. in Sociology, with a minor in Psychology; an M.A. in Guidance and Counseling; and an Ed.D. in Adult Education, with a focus in sociology and gerontology. I also spent two years in the Peace Corps in Tehran, Iran, as an urban social worker at Tehran University. In addition, I have worked for the Human Development Institute subsidiary of Bell & Howell in Atlanta, Georgia, as a human relations consultant and have been a college counselor and adjunct professor for more than 35 years.

I have developed counseling specialties in grief and loss, disabilities, alcohol and other drug abuse, diversity awareness, intuitive awareness, anti-racism, sexism and ageism, and trust building. My dissertation research, "Correlating Interpersonal Trust Scores with Life Satisfaction Scores of Older Adults," stimulated my interest in working with older women even more. In my research, I found a positive relationship between trust and life satisfaction in older adults (Hofsess 1980). My innate passion for these issues coupled with the data from my research led me to make contact with the local senior center in Corning, New York, which is where in 1993 the first TLOW group was started.

Some have asked me why I only focus on older women and not older individuals in general. I decided to focus on older women, even though older men also benefit from trust groups, because I wanted to start with some early success and older women generally are more receptive to being in a support group experience than older men. In addition, women outlive men, often live alone and in isolation, and are traditionally major caregivers. For these reasons, it seemed they would be a group who would readily benefit from support. Helping them, in turn, has benefits to their entire family system and their communities as a whole.

Creating an atmosphere of trust is at the core of this work and is key to the success of these groups. Trust is what enables these women to be supportive and caring to one another, which is fundamental in helping them reap the benefits of the support group environment. Women members often report a variety of physical and mental health benefits, as well as interpersonal and social benefits, that carry over to their daily lives in their communities.

There are 12 established in upstate New York, and my goal is to eventually see one in every community—not just in New York State but nationwide and even internationally. Sponsoring agencies of these groups are churches, senior centers, YWCAs, YMCAs, college alumni associations, and residential-living facilities. Agencies interested in establishing a TLOW group send representatives to a day-long facilitator training workshop. The representative then becomes the primary facilitator of a TLOW group for the respective agency. With the help of these types of community organizations, older women benefit from the sense of community these groups provide.

One primary purpose of this book is to bring attention to the marginalization of older women, and another is to offer some insight into and information about this often overlooked population. Although I emphasize one strategy to minimize the marginalization of older women, the development of TLOW groups, I am invested in highlighting all that can be done to create a social support structure for this demographic. I strive to bring attention and respect to this group of very special individuals. My passion for the TLOW idea has evolved from my earliest beginnings.

As a way of sharing my work and engaging in dialog with other professionals working with older women, I have presented the TLOW concept and training material at professional conferences—including the International Federation on Ageing conferences in Singapore (2004), Copenhagen (2006), and Montreal (2008). Delegates from around the world

(Africa, Asia, Europe, North America, South America, and Australia) have attended my sessions and have indicated that the ideas behind TLOW have cross-cultural transferability. The feedback I have received informs me that TLOW groups are ready to be started in other regions of the world.

In closing, my editor and I thank you for taking the time to read about this very important work.

—*Ron Hofsess*

Corning, New York
October 2012

⫟ ACKNOWLEDGMENTS ⫟

⫟⫟⫟⫟ ⫟ ⫟⫟⫟⫟

I extend a deep and abiding appreciation to Clay Hofsess, my father, and Beulah Hofsess, my mother, for exposing me to the lives of older people and for modeling sensitivity to their needs. With humility, I also thank my sisters Helen, Margaret, Virginia, and Annette for directly and indirectly teaching me to be sensitive to females when I was a boy growing up. I thank my daughter and coauthor Christy for continuing to help me maintain that sensitivity through her warmth and directness, and my son Jason for his love and support.

I thank my dear friends Merle Hutchinson, Donna Hutchinson, Diane Breton, Priscilla Crispell, Penny Duffy, Lorraine Gibb, Wilma Beaman, and Margaret Whittaker for their wisdom and insights into the value of creating communities of trust for older women.

With gratitude, I thank the women in the Trust in the Lives of Older Women's Group from the Corning Senior Center in Corning, New York; and the women in the Elmira College group; and Christy Balliett, Peggy Arnesen, Mila Meier, Linda Tetor, and Kathy Burns for the leadership roles they played in encouraging these and other groups to exist and thrive.

I wish to express my thanks to Angela Graefe for her editorial assistance, and to Daril Bentley for his copyediting, editorial and publishing guidance, assemblage and design of the manuscript and cover, and contribution of poems to the edition.

I would also like to mention friends in the world of government who have been supportive of the Trust in the Lives of Older Women movement. These friends have included a few members of Congress representing my hometown: Amo Houghton, Randy Kuhl, Eric Massa, and Tom Reed. I have also enjoyed support from local officials, including three mayors of Corning: Jim Bacallas, later to be a state assemblyman; Tom Reed, who went on to Congress; and Rich Negri. Their support has been invaluable. In fact, Congressman Tom Reed has stated that he would like to see this model available to anyone in the country who might have a need for it.

And I have a very special place in my heart for my dearest and beloved friend, Dorothy West, who taught me many things—especially to appreciate what I have.

⭍ Introduction ⭍

ⅲⅲ ⅲⅲ ⅲⅲ ⅲⅲ ⭍ ⅲⅲ ⅲⅲ ⅲⅲ ⅲⅲ

This book documents the ways in which older women are marginalized, and suggests a framework for empowering them to come together with their sisters to take control of their own fates. Although there are many older women who live enriched and fulfilled lives, this book is geared toward acknowledging the plight of those who for myriad reasons (explored throughout) have been relegated to a position in society where marginalization is the norm. Nonetheless, older women are still major contributors to their families and communities in spite of this marginalization. In Chapter 1, we offer some rather sobering statistics and information regarding older women and the obstacles they often face. Poverty, lack of community resources to support their needs, the stress of being a caregiver, and poor self-image are just a few of these obstacles. Older women must deal with many unique and challenging issues and situations that affect their daily lives, in addition to the inevitable difficulties associated with normal aging.

Aging is a process. It occurs at different rates for various individuals, depending on their group, gender, and culture. Aging encompasses a broad spectrum of experiences that are influenced by genetics, anxieties, and exposure to environmental, social, and economic stimuli. Societies assign age expectations according to gender, sociocultural norms, and role assignments.

The aging process begins before birth and continues throughout life. The body's biological systems develop rapidly during the first years of life, reach their peak in early adulthood, and gradually decline thereafter. For women, these developmental stages can be further categorized to encompass their physical and social development. Female development begins in the womb, and then continues during the first six years of life and through adolescence—the interval between being in school and entry into the workforce. Young adulthood is often followed by motherhood and middle age, which brings issues related to menopause—and at times the introduction of chronic illnesses. The last phase of life is often widowhood for many women (World Health Organization). The slope and speed of aging are often influenced and sometimes directly determined by lifestyle choices, environment, and other external factors. As a result, health in old age is often seen as a reflection of circumstances and actions experienced during one's entire life span.

Women's psychological disposition and social observance also influence the way they age. In Chapter 2, we discuss the importance of social connections and the role that support, community, and other groups play in women's lives. In addition to social support, coping style determines how well one adapts to changes such as retirement and negative life events such as illness and bereavement (Baltes and Baltes 1990, p. 26). Optimism and a sense of stability are also positively linked to mental and social well-being as one ages. The "contagion effect" helps explain that social networks can have a direct impact on a community's sense of life satisfaction and overall happiness (Christakis and Fowler 2009).

According to the World Health Organization, active aging also depends on a person's ability to maintain meaning in life despite personal losses, physical decline, and ageism. Some studies show that many older women, particularly older women of color, rely on prayer and faith as a means of coping with losses associated with aging (Wong 1998 in WHO 2007, p. 26). Faith often provides consolation and strength and serves as a guide for daily living.

Chapter 3 offers one possible solution to the perception and actuality of isolation that many older women experience. For many older women, self-esteem is fragile, health is compromised, and social resources are limited. Support groups such as Trust in the Lives of Older Women (TLOW) can fill the void and address some of the needs facing older women. (See Chapter 3 for more on TLOW and its definition of "trust.")

In the 2007 report issued by the World Health Organization (WHO 2007, p.36), many social influences were identified as impacting the aging process. These include education and literacy, violence and abuse, social exclusion, human rights, social support, and empowerment. For example, people with a low level of education have shorter life spans and poorer overall health than people with a higher level of education. Some studies have shown that this disparity in health expectancy is greater in women than in men (Bossuyt et al. 2003; Manor et al. 2004). Worldwide, illiteracy is very high among women aged 60 and older—which limits their ability to be active citizens and members of their society. Involvement in social support groups can help minimize the negative impact these and other influences have on quality of life.

Chapter 4 highlights testimonials of individuals involved in TLOW groups, with representatives from respected agencies and organizations endorsing the benefits of TLOW groups. Actual participants of TLOW groups also offer their feedback and praise, expressing their gratitude regarding the impact their involvement in these groups has had on their lives.

In Chapter 5, we offer suggestions for improving and increasing the resources needed to help this population overcome its often-poor living conditions, low income, and minimal social outlets. Expanded programs and increased support are essential in helping older women maintain a minimum standard of living.

According to the World Health Organization (WHO, p. 3), "Ageing [*sic*] women make up a significant proportion of the world's population and their numbers are growing." The organization's document also makes the following observations. In older age groups, women outnumber men—and the imbalance increases with age. The fastest-growing subgroup among the aging are women over the age of 80. Worldwide, there are approximately 189 women for every 100 men aged 80 and older.

There is a significant need for support for this demographic. When we consider all of the unrecognized contributions and sacrifices older women make in their lifetimes to their families and communities, the need for increased resources becomes undeniable.

In Chapter 6, we share some personal thoughts regarding the evolution of the TLOW groups and what we think they contribute to the quality of life for their participants. As these groups expand, more women will benefit from their support and the trusting environment they provide. The increased quality of life of older women can then positively impact the families and communities for whom they care.

ᴵ INTRODUCTORY POEMS ON MATURE LIFE ᴹ

—By Daril Bentley

Dedicated to Wanda White—daughter, sister, wife,
mother, friend, businesswoman, community supporter
and volunteer, and TLOW Group Leader

✿✿✿✿✿✿✿✿✿

Yellow Sweater

I watch from a second-story window
my white-haired neighbor
in a yellow cotton sweater raking yellow
maple leaves in the courtyard.
The landlord is surely not paying her

To tidy up the grounds.
Perhaps she simply desires to relive,
to reclaim, days spent in happiness
around the house with her late husband.
Do not think it is hard

Of me that I do not rush down to assist.
Some acts are sacrosanct of privacy
in the temple of human bounds.
Her rake is the comb she drew gently
through his silver hair at the last.

Nothing I could give
to her or say to her could curse or bless
her passage from this land.
No, I will not lift a finger
to yank her back from yellow memory

To this lifeless landscape of dark art.
No, I will not intervene or resist.
When I am dotard, I will stuff a pillow
with leaves. All the tenants of my heart
will wear a yellow sweater.

Testaments to the Western Elders

The igneous fingerlike monoliths of Monument Valley;
a shag-cedar stave gate at Nambé, New Mexico;
the exposed adobe of a seventeenth-century mission
and the grizzled cottonwood that looked on then
and is looking on now; a hail-battered tin roof

That looks like the embattled scales of an old dragon
too tired now to roam and ravage the countryside;
the plank I of a general store, Ouray, Colorado;
the chipped yellow brick of city hall, Tombstone;
the chimneys and stovepipes of Leadville;

A slowly eroding pumice-pocked prehistoric lava flow;
the twisted barn-board sidewalk from entry
to the old miner's property up to the curling floor
of the porch; the snakeskin gouged and discolored hide
of the sash around the windows and the front door

Of a homestead falling back into the earth at Flagstaff;
the curved and listing creosoted telephone pole
along the dirt main street blowing away with the wind
in Price and Deming and Brownsville and Silverton;
tar paper held by a single rusted two-penny nail

To the side of an outhouse in Animas Forks;
the horns of wooly winter billy goats scavenging
leafless salt cedar and huddling near the Pecos River;
the gravestones carved with rising spirits at Tesuque
and the wooden ones warping in the long buffalo

Grass at Questa and Kansas City and Pollard's Find;
the dust-dimmed factory plate-glass panes of a window
biding their time as the old house falls in around them;
the rusting hulls of nineteen-twenties Ford trucks
taking it easy now on the ranch no one works anymore;

The sign that points toward the Ortiz Mountains
that reads Have You Seen America? and Petrified
Forest and Visit the Only Turquoise Mine Working;
the mesa shorn flat by wind and passing storm
over the course of millennia, before ever a living soul

First wandered down from the Neolithic ice sheet; gray
horse skull, mule deer skull, cattle skull, and elk skull;
miles of folded-dough fingernail-file bentonite that goad
imagination within the Heartnut Desert and at Hanksville;
Anasazi ruin, Mummy Cave, Canyon del Muerto,

Utah, and the empty endless reach of the searing plains
baking the new grass above the old scorched-brown
dead grass in the summer sun; twisted cedar-tree bole
aging into the driftwood of the white water
of the quartz sands south of Carlsbad and Alamagordo:

These are all testament to our debt to the old men
and the old women who came before and who still
move and do and love and endure among us. These are
all the explanation for their leathered and cracked skin,
their burnished exteriors made resilient and rugged

By their knowledge slowly tempered into wisdom.
These are the documents and the claim stakes that show
they changed this place utterly forever for having been.
These are the National Registry of Historical
Deeds and Dreams and Triumphs and Failures recorded

In the farm machinery and the bridge of iron and steel
and the stone and the wrinkled tree bark along the road.
These are their names carved in the macadam.
These are the markers of their beauties and their tender
ways and their light, as if the setting sun required proof.

Barbed Wire

Barbed wire should not long be new,
should not shine,
should not be inflexible—not
strung post to post
as stridently as a youngster goes.

Barbed wire should be rust
red, should sag
where the children and the hunters
have gone over it
over the years.

Nor should this or that face of late
I prefer to view
be smooth and taut,
nor unblemished,
nor unridden-down with cares.

A face should wear lime dust
and a grizzled mane
shaken across its ashen furrows,
should be a nag
if you need it done right you turn to.

The eyes become wires
in such a face—hot
to the foolish and the unjust,
useful old barbed wire to those
whose judgment bears some weight.

For the Realtor

I require that house with a willow tree
and the scent of cut grass.
When I go up the stairs

I want there to be
a round cupola with windows round
overlooking the lawn.

There I will make my brown study
looking out upon the willow.
There I will write grants for the grass

Until the leaves all
turn brown and turn
and gracefully forgive the ground.

I want a house with an old stone wall
I can let go
to the saxifrage and the ivy,

To the summer rains and the moss,
when I go up the stairs
to turn toward a room I do not know.

EMERGING FROM THE SHADOWS

*The Needs of Older Women
and the Benefits of Supporting Them*

1

AGING
AND
OLDER WOMEN

*"Loneliness and the feeling of being
unwanted is the most terrible poverty."*

—Mother Teresa, Winner of the Nobel Peace Prize, 1979

ﬔﬔ ﬔﬔ ﬔﬔ ﬔﬔ ﬔ ﬔﬔ ﬔﬔ ﬔﬔ ﬔﬔ

Aging is a process none of us can avoid or stop. Along with its inevitability, it potentially brings to the table an air of distinction as seen in the form of maturity, wisdom, and respect. But because of its pervasiveness it also brings disappointment in the form of physical, social, economic, and often emotional deterioration. Society often devalues the aging process and, as a consequence, older people.

Despite varying global cultures and mores, perceptions of the aged range from positive traits such as "sweet, pleasant, wise, giving, and caring" to such negative characteristics such as "slow, cranky, and repetitive" (Schenk and Achenbaum 1994, p. ix). The elderly are often neatly categorized into such dichotomous stereotypes, but older women in particular are commonly stereotyped negatively and thus have experiences that engender disappointment and discrimination in many forms.

Women Among the Elderly

The elderly are a diverse group. Diversity abounds in this age group in both developed and developing countries, reflecting differences in gender, class, race, ethnicity, and culture. Based on these differences, there is a great deal of variability among the elderly in terms of values, customs, beliefs and practices, religious leanings, political views, level of education, and overall well-being. Although they share common situational characteristics—such as limited access to economic resources, care and services, and illness—"the elderly are more individually distinct than any other segment of the population" (Gurlanik et al. 1991).

Older women in particular face many challenges, including the loss of family and friends, being caregivers for others, and living alone. If married,

1

it is likely a woman will outlive her husband. A woman's life expectancy averages 79 years, whereas a man's averages 74 years. The following statistics are from the 2010 U.S. Census.

❖ Women age 65 and older living alone: 37%

❖ Men age 65 and older living alone: 19%

This tells us that nearly twice the number of women age 65 and older compared to men of the same age live alone. The same statistical data also tells us that there are 8.1 million women age 75 or older who live alone in non-institutionalized settings compared to 3.2 million men of the same age group. We can see from these statistics that more women continue to live alone than men as they age.

Ethnicity in the United States is also a variable that has an impact on the well-being of older women. The difference in life expectancy between ethnic minority women and women of European American descent is approximately five years. Women of African American heritage have the highest mortality rates, and those of Asian and Pacific Islander descent have the lowest mortality rates of all racial/ethnic groups. Native American women experience slightly higher mortality rates than European American women between the ages of 55 and 64, but have lower mortality rates thereafter (Torrez 1997).

On a global level, women's life expectancy is shorter when their status is very low and when their access to basic resources such as food or health care is drastically reduced. Life expectancy is also impacted when women eat less and lower-quality food, are exposed to complications from frequent childbearing and sexually transmitted diseases, and experience restricted access to modern health care (Unger 2001, p. 193).

Lack of Research

Because of the lack of research on older women, very little is known about how decisions about life-extending care are made—and even less on how being an older woman affects these decisions. What is known is based on research done on older men—largely having to do with how they differ from older women not only related to factors affecting death but quality of life.

Changes in living arrangements, psychological well-being in mid and old age, decision-making, and retirement have been examined as they relate to the older man. However, these and other issues involving older women have not been studied nearly as much.

The available research on older women is limited (Garner and Mercer 2001, p. 54), which further demonstrates how they are often marginalized. Their usefulness is too often minimized, and they are seen as unusable; that is, they aren't even valued as research subjects. This trend is reflected in the psychological literature as well, in which until the 1970s and 1980s most research and theory about psychological development was focused on men and male development (Gilligan 1993).

Poor Self-image

Older women's identities are frequently distorted by negative social images that devalue them, making them feel invisible and insignificant (Butler 1969). Their vulnerability becomes heightened, and they can begin to see themselves as helpless and frail rather than as strong and capable. This cycle of negative perceptions is self-perpetuating.

The marginalization of older women begins at birth. Despite the progress made from the efforts of the feminist movement, sexism persists. Consequently, females are often seen as less valuable to families, communities, and societies than males. This bias can be seen in their early conditioning regarding subservient roles, which may lead to fewer opportunities to access resources for their further development. Although prejudicial thinking has been changing in some societies, it is still a prevalent attitude in our global community. For example, in the United States many young girls have been limited and still are limited in their development of math and science mastery—which results in a more narrow selection of academic study and fewer career opportunities.

L. S. Gottfredson (1981, 1996), in her developmental theory of career aspirations, refers to the process by which children narrow their career choices as "circumscription." Kids narrow their "zone of acceptable career alternatives" based on the sex-appropriateness of a particular occupation, the occupation's social prestige, and their own perceived abilities to succeed in the career.

For instance, in college-level math anxiety courses that Ron Hofsess taught more than 90% of his students were females. Most of them recounted how well they did in arithmetic and math earlier in their lives, as they shared their math histories. However, often in middle school and the first few years of high school many of them described how they were ridiculed, teased, and even discouraged from excelling in math. This often resulted in an internal conflict and subsequent anxiety that may have interfered with their math performance. It is usually this type of math history that leads these females into a math anxiety class or away from math altogether.

There are many societal factors that may contribute to older women's poor self-image. "The media and prevailing attitudes often portray men as ageing [sic] with wisdom, while women become 'invisible' in middle-age and viewed as a burden in older age. This disadvantage is, in part, due to a tendency to equate women's worth with beauty, youth, and reproduction" (WHO 2007, p. 37). In addition, older women are often glossed over for positions of leadership at all levels: community, national, and international. This is particularly evident with older women who are poor. Economic and social status directly correlates with the frequency of and interaction with social, political, and economic participation—whether on an individual or group basis.

In many countries in the world, women's primary involvement is still thought of as procreation, housework, and caregiving—all unpaid occupations. These activities often prevent women from pursuing education, viable employment opportunities, and skill building. Part-time, low-paying employment and insignificant jobs that offer few benefits set the pattern that many older women find themselves locked into. Even in the United States, they still earn less than their male counterparts and experience inequality at work and at home.

Historically in many societies throughout the world, male offspring were and still are preferred over females. So, the early message to young females is that they will have access to fewer resources compared to males—and this is played out in the extreme as they age. Age and gender function as a system of social classification. These aspects of identity determine a person's location on the social map in-terms of power, status, and access to resources (Unger 2001, p. 184). Older women are perceived as nice but unattractive and dull, and are often viewed as less competent, intelligent, wise, and independent than older men (Canetto et al. 1995). They are also more likely to be pitied than celebrated for their longevity (Unger 2001, p. 196). As they age, older women must try to maintain a positive view of the self while society increasingly communicates a negative message about their value.

Finally, being robbed of choice-making undermines an older woman's self-concept. For example, in some countries inheritance laws and practices discriminate against women. Under certain legal systems, daughters inherit half as much as their brothers—and mothers inherit less than their children. When a husband dies, the widow can retain custody of her children. However, "the children's legal guardianship goes to the relatives of the deceased father" (Hoskins 1991). The guardian, not the mother, gets to control the children's property and wealth.

The Caregiver Role

Older women are typically involved in a variety of caregiving activities for their husbands, significant others, children, parents, grandchildren, other relatives, and friends. For some, such a role continues for several decades. However, caregiving impinges on women's already limited resources, often leading to emotional, physical, and economic strain. Unger (p. 194) observes, given the longstanding perception that reproductive and caregiving work are women's life vocation:

> *...women's lives may be seen as complete but meaningless when they can no longer function as caregivers. Sick, older women who need (rather than provide) caregiving may be particularly vulnerable to seeing themselves, and to be viewed by others, as burdensome.*

Social contact and self-care may be reduced due to task overload (Unger, 189). When they become ill, they receive less help from family and friends. Yet, the gendered stereotype of women's self-sacrifice reinforces their perception of themselves as a burden—which is how they are treated by others.

Although the caregiving role can be a burden on older women, a study at Johns Hopkins University showed that the experience can also reap rewards: "Children are more likely to receive better grades and are less likely to suffer injuries under a grandparent's care." The term *grandma effect* has been coined

5

by the researchers to describe this benefit from grandparent care (Global Action on Aging, Nov. 10, 2008).

Prevalence of Poverty

Poverty among older women is multidimensional, not just economic. When one thinks of poverty, the first thing that may come to mind is having little or no income—with very slim prospects of economic improvement. But poverty takes on many shapes and forms.

First, there's social poverty—in which one is alone many days and has little social contact or interaction with friends, family and, often, even neighbors. "More than 1 million pensioners said they nearly always feel lonely; they felt like prisoners in their homes because they could not get out without assistance" (Global Action on Aging, Oct. 31, 2008). Intellectual poverty exists when there is little opportunity to interact with others by way of sharing one's history and the knowledge one has acquired from life experiences or education. In contrast, it can also take on the shape of ignorance and illiteracy.

In addition, there is poverty of health. As women age, their physical health and well-being may be compromised. Without the proper resources and support systems, older women's health can quickly deteriorate. So, not only can specific forms of poverty affect the well-being of older women but any combination of factors—such as "low income, poor health, age-based discrimination, reduced physical or mental capacity, isolation, abuse, limited access to health and long-term care services" (Global Action on Aging, Oct. 17, 2008)— impacts the increase in poverty and exclusion of women as they age.

Older women's poverty is a problem internationally as well. According to data from the International Council on Social Welfare (Sadik 1997), "many older women are unable to meet their minimal needs for nutrition and shelter." Everywhere in the world, "poverty has a female face" (Unger 2001, p. 186). The multilayered inequalities that women experience during their lifetime because of their gender, class, race, ethnicity, and marital status very often place them in conditions of poverty. In some countries, special limitations are applied to widows but not to widowers.

In the article "The World's Women 1995: Trends and Statistics," published by the United Nations, upper-caste widows in India are not allowed to work and must live in their deceased husband's residence under restriction of diet, dress, and demeanor. In parts of Papua New Guinea, older widows were ritually killed by their kin because they were considered a burden to their children. "Widowers, however, were not treated as a burden, and were not ritually killed" (Canetto and Lester 1998). Worldwide, widows are a larger and older group than widowers—and although most cultures encourage men to remarry (often to younger women) widows experience a strong social stigma if they remarry. Of the proportion of women aged 65 or older, widows constitute 75% in the Republic of Korea, 71% in Morocco, 70% in India, 61% in Japan, 59% in Hungary, 44% in Switzerland, 35% in Cuba, and 32% in Haiti (United Nations Centre 1991).

In Canada, the number of homeless baby boomers has increased among women over age 55. Researchers warn that as people continue to age homelessness among the elderly will continue to be an issue (Global Action on Aging, Sept. 18, 2008). Unger, citing Sadik (pp. 5–7), states:

According to data from the International Council on Social Welfare, women's poverty around the world is due to gender discrimination in education, employment, and access to economic resources (such as credit, land ownership, and inheritance property), as well as women's under-representation in political decision-making.

One of the biggest fears about retirement that 46% of single women report is that they will outlive their money. According to the Ninth Annual Transamerica Retirement Survey, elderly women are more likely to live in poverty. Marital status is a critical factor affecting poverty in retirement (Global Action on Aging, Sept. 17, 2008). For example, a single widow is more likely to live in poverty than her married counterpart. In addition to the reduced income that results from the death of one's spouse, widows in some cultures are subjected to social stigma, taboos, and restrictions that are harmful to their mental and physical health. For example, "…the approximately 33 million widows in India are expected to lead chaste, isolated, and austere lives" (Who 2007, p. 36).

Older women who live alone as a result of divorce or loss of a spouse are more likely to experience higher levels of poverty and to be institutionalized than those who live with family members. They are also more likely to feel depressed or isolated, and require aid from state services such as home help (WHO 2007, p. 40). To compound their isolation, they are often discriminated against simply because of their age and gender.

Economic Conditions and Concerns

Older women who once focused on taking care of the home instead of having a job outside the home are left without pensions in their later years. Widows appear to be suffering the most. In June of 2008, Congress approved a proposition to increase widows' pensions to help improve their living conditions.

All over the world, pension funds are affected by economic fluctuations. Poland, for example, lost approximately half its open pension funds in 2008. Such dramatic losses will be felt most by people retiring soon; there is little time for the funds to regenerate. Women generally retire five years earlier than men, leaving them with less money in their pension funds. The impact of the economic downturn will affect them even more (Global Action on Aging, Oct. 27, 2008).

Another economic concern involves funding of state programs. For example, in 2008 North Carolina anticipated withholding $2 million in funding for Meals on Wheels and other programs essential for the well-being of disabled and older persons. Cuts in funding impact older persons (many of them low-income females), who rely on in-home aides and home-delivered meals. These types of programs help this demographic maintain its independence, and funding cuts deleteriously impact women's ability to live independently (Global Action on Aging, Nov. 10, 2008).

Limitations in Health Care

As mentioned previously, clinical studies often focus on the older male experience, leaving a large gap in research regarding the gender differences in the aging process and their effects on health and social well-being. Older women "suffer from more ill health and disabilities than older men, but have fewer resources to deal with their health problems" (Unger 2001, p. 196). Because older women live longer, they experience their physical decline for a longer period—and their health issues are often more severe than men's (Unger 2001, p. 184).

According to a report issued by the World Health Organization, aging women do not have the same access to health care as do men or even younger women. And the older a woman gets, the greater the barriers to primary health care become evident. Such barriers include lack of transportation, lack of money to pay for medications and services, and low literacy levels. As women live longer, they are less likely to have health insurance coverage and as a result are also more likely to exhaust their financial resources on health-related expenses (Hess 1990). Discrimination in treatment becomes more and more likely with the presence of these barriers.

The situation for some older women can become desperate. In China, for example, suicide is more common in women than in men—especially in rural areas, where 90% of the suicides occur. As far back as 1999, statistics show that 50% of all suicides by women in the world occurred in China.

Impact of War/Trauma

In war-devastated Iraq, many seniors—especially women—are vulnerable. According to Global Action on Aging (June 27, 2007), "Traditionally dependent upon relatives and extended family care, Baghdad's older population is being abandoned in greater numbers as relatives flee the violence and chaos of Iraq."

In Tanzania, more than 1,000 killings of older women occur annually. Murders of older women are not only tolerated but accepted. If older women outlive their own children who have succumbed to the AIDS epidemic, they are regarded with suspicion and often accused of witchcraft. According to Global Action on Aging (Dec. 1–5, 2008), "Widows in Tanzania are particularly voiceless having low status in a society and no knowledge about their own rights."

In Spain, the mistreatment of older persons is on the rise. Roughly 72% of the victims, the majority of whom are women, live with their aggressors—who in many cases are their partners. The victims suffer from negligence; they "are not cared for in a respectful manner and their needs are not met" (Global Action on Aging, Oct. 22, 2008).

The Unrecognized Value of Older Women

According to Mary Jo Gibson and Ari N. Housen of the AARP Public Policy Institute, the 2007 economic value of unpaid caregivers' contributions to the

United States was estimated to be $350 billion. The argument can be made that the U.S. government must give better support to family caregivers to maintain the health care system, long-term care system, and the economy (AARP 2007). Title III(e) funding, which provides respite assistance for caregivers, is an example of government support for this demographic. According to Worell and Goodheart (p. 394), "Communities that are responsive to aging women will find that these elders are also a potential market for local business and a source of loyal and hard-working employees."

Older women are big contributors to the global economy. According to the World Health Organization, they "...do between two-thirds and three-quarters of the work in the world. They also produce 45% of the world's food. But they are still granted only 10% of the world's income and 1% of the world's property" (French 1992, p. 30). Their work comprises a lifetime of experience and learned expertise. They represent approximately 25% of the economically active older workforce (United Nations 1995b). However, in parts of Europe early retirement policies encourage older women to withdraw from the workforce permanently. In some countries in the Middle East, the number of older women in the workforce is lower than in other developing regions.

In many parts of the world, older women offer their services as unpaid contributors in the form of mentors, volunteers, historians, fund-raisers, and of course, caregivers. Many receive no financial compensation for their efforts. For example, in Jordan less than 1% of older women work for a wage. For some women who are economically secure, this arrangement is perfectly acceptable—but for most a regular income could make the difference between being considered poverty level or just above it (Jacobs 1993, p. 191).

According to the World Health Organization, "Ageing [sic] women make an important contribution to the socioeconomic well-being of their families, communities, and nations" (WHO 2007, p. 32). As mentioned previously, many older women work in caregiving, child-rearing, volunteer, and domestic types of work situations—making a valuable contribution to the well-being of their families and communities. Current trends indicate that the number of women raising grandchildren will continue to increase. Women who care for their grandchildren because of drug addiction, abuse, AIDS, or incarceration of their own children often experience great economic hardships. They give up jobs, retirement plans, church activities, and social lives to become parents a second time (Garner and Mercer 2001, p. 122).

In Africa and other areas seriously affected by the widespread prevalence of HIV/AIDS, older women also serve an increasingly important role in the financial and emotional support of their family's households. Unfortunately, discrimination in wages and pension policies severely hurts older women and their ability not only to care for those in their charge but to care for themselves when no one else (including themselves) is able to care for them.

Supporting Those Overlooked

It is extremely important that older women have access to very basic services, such as food, potable water, shelter, primary health care, and—perhaps the most easily overlooked—social support. Support must be provided for those in a caregiver role. A mix of public and private sources of income in old age would help older women fulfill and continue their caregiving roles, as well as help those families who care for older women and men who are unable to live independently (WHO 2007, p. 34).

The quality of life of older women in many ways depends on being able to build new, trusting relationships in their increasingly isolated environments. To do this, these women need support. Policies, programs, and practices need to "take into account the special situations of older women with disabilities, members of minority groups, those who live in rural areas, and those who have low socioeconomic status" (WHO 2007, p. 7). By assisting older women who live in poor and/or rural areas, the needs of the world's poorest people will also be met because this population depends so much on the care and attention provided by the older women in their lives.

Instituting programs geared toward helping older women navigate the problems they face as they age can provide significant cost savings in human and financial resources. When environmental conditions are favorable and affordable, and need-specific services are available, the aging process is more likely to increase one's life satisfaction. Older women can contribute more readily to volunteer opportunities, and they can continue to contribute to the welfare of others. These benefits have a positive domino effect on their community, on the recipients' situation, and on society in general. Social support and social interaction help improve an older woman's self-esteem, her sense of empowerment, and her pleasure with being considered a viable and appreciated member of society.

These outcomes help mitigate against stress and minimize the effects of traumatic events in older women's lives. Recipients and givers both benefit when resources are made available to older women because they can continue doing what they have always been drawn to do or simply expected to do. When society appreciates the contributions older women have made to the welfare of family, friends, and community members, women become honored for the lifelong contributions they have made. They are valued and seen as visible treasures. Older women could then begin to see themselves as people with something of value to give, instead of as burdens—as they are too often labeled by their families and by society.

Appendix E contains many examples of older women who achieved great things and made many valuable contributions to society, inspiring the children of their generation and of the generations that followed. The following are just a sampling of these noteworthy women, their accomplishments, and their contributions.

Emily Green Balch

Emily Green Balch (1867 – 1961) was an American political scientist, socialist, economist, social reformer, and pacifist. She was a leader of the women's movement for peace during World War I. She helped establish the Women's International League for Peace and Freedom in 1919 (at age 52), and was the group's secretary-treasurer from 1934 to 1935 (at age 67). She continued promoting peace throughout her life, sharing the Nobel Peace Prize in 1946 (at age 79) with John Raleigh Mott (age 81) and writing *Toward Human Unity* in 1952 (at age 85).

Tilly Edinger

Tilly Edinger, vertebrate paleontologist, was named president of the Society of Vertebrate Paleontology when she was 66. She is considered to have virtually established the field of paleo-neurology (the study of fossil brains).

Ella Deloria

Ella Deloria (1889 – 1971), a Yankton Sioux Native American linguist and author, was a true keeper of her culture. She translated thousands of pages of ethnographic texts written in the Sioux language and compiled a Lakota (a dialect of the Sioux) grammar and dictionary. At the age of 73, in conjunction with the University of South Dakota's Institute for Indian Studies, she received a large National Science Foundation grant to compile a Sioux dictionary. She continued working on her dictionary, publishing articles and lecturing, until shortly before her death at age 82. Her activities played a significant role in ensuring the survival and continued strength of the Sioux.

Sister Gertrude Morgan

At the age of 39, Sister Gertrude Morgan (1900 – 1980)—in partnership with two other women—started an orphanage (Gentilly) in New Orleans. She devoted herself to this work, which she saw as her mission in life. The orphanage grew, thrived, and made a tremendous contribution to the community thanks to Sister Gertrude's efforts. However, in 1965—when Sister Gertrude was 65—tragedy struck: Hurricane Betsy swept through New Orleans, destroying the orphanage.

Confronted with a devastating void in her life, Sister Gertrude began to do more of the painting she had begun when she was 56. In her seventies, her art reached maturity, and museums across the country began to exhibit it in recognition of her prodigious talent. Her work was included in the 1980 exhibit of the Corcoran Museum of Art on "Black Folk Art in America."

Fusae Ichikawa

Fusae Ichikawa (1893 – 1981), the Japanese feminist and politician, formed the Women's Suffrage League in Japan in 1924—and following World War II became head of the new Japan Women's League, which in 1945 secured the right for women to vote. From 1952 to 1971 (when she was age 78), she served in the National Diet of Japan—fighting for wider women's rights and battling different forms of corruption. After defeat in 1971, she triumphantly returned to parliament in 1975 (at age 82)—where she continued to serve until age 87.

CHAPTER

2

COMMUNITY
AND
CONNECTION

Places of Worship

Senior Centers

Senior Housing

"It's so clear that you have to cherish everyone. I think that's what I get from these older black women, that every soul is to be cherished, that every flower is to bloom."

**—Alice Walker, novelist and winner of the
Pulitzer Prize for Fiction, 1983**

ᛀᛀᛀ ᛀᛀᛀ ᛀᛀᛀ ᛀᛀᛀ ᛱ ᛀᛀᛀ ᛀᛀᛀ ᛀᛀᛀ ᛀᛀᛀ

The importance of community and connection in women's lives cannot be overestimated. A woman's belief that she is "valued, loved, and an integral part of a social relationship" is a major factor in her overall well-being (Shearer and Fleury 2006). Support can be defined as preventing something bad from happening and thus causing something good to happen. It means that something positive is given to the recipient to aid their cause or interests, which results in a positive outcome of some type that strengthens and maintains well-being.

Social support and interactions with others help maintain overall good health. Research demonstrates that personal friendships are essential for individuals to recover from life tragedies (Gannon 1999; Garner & Mercer 2001). The opportunity to share one's hurt, despair, grief, and loss are critical in the healing process. Yet for so many older women quality social support is limited.

Inadequate Support

Older women, particularly those who live in rural areas, often turn to different sources of support—depending on their need and the length of time support is required. For example, Coward and Krout report in a study that family members were turned to for short-term assistance, whereas formal support was favored when there was a need for longer-term ongoing assistance (Coward and Krout 1998, p. 160). Data from 1990 showed that regardless of their geographic location approximately 25% of rural and urban older women were similar in that they "did not have persons within their social networks that they could call on for help or to discuss personal matters" (Coward and Krout 1998, p. 156).

Older women are included less and less in our communities and in society as a whole. Their social network is gradually disappearing through deaths of family members and friends. They and/or their friends move away. Fewer people are available from their usual social network for them to connect with. Other social networks in their community—such as recreational groups, informal employee gatherings, and clubs and associations—have fewer and fewer older women and as a consequence do not include the older women in their world. These social networks sometimes forget that older women exist.

Benefits of Social Outlets

Research has shown that when women get together the level of a hormone called oxytocin increases (Taylor et al., 2000). People with higher levels of oxytocin are more likely to trust others, are more resistant to stress and phobias, and bond more easily with others (Brooks 1969). Having positive social outlets and opportunities to establish supportive relationships has become increasingly valuable to the overall well-being of older women.

Lowered stress levels, stronger friendships, and increased trust levels encourage community building and strengthen the benefits obtained from such social interactions. Older women who seek out opportunities for support and sources of encouragement tend to suffer less from depression. Fostering the creation of bonding groups for older women benefits not only the women but their families and communities.

Meaning/Spirituality

Being a valued member of a congregation or religious group is a viable and frequent source of social support and increases self-esteem (Mollard 1995). If an older woman lives alone and is unable to leave her home because of disabilities, having access to pastoral care and counseling can be very helpful. In addition to providing spiritual input, churches and religious groups "can be an important source of social support, validation, hope, and reassurance that her life and death have meaning" (WHO 2007, p. 26).

Some studies conducted by the National Institute on Aging show that social networks promote happiness in older people. Connecting with family and friends affects health and happiness, and influences longevity (Global Action on Aging, June 24, 2009).

Lower Mortality Rates

Participation in social networks has also had a protective and positive effect on mortality. In a 1997 study published in the *American Journal of Epidemiology*, it was found that both age and specific aspects of network structures influenced the connection between social groups and mortality in older women. For instance, women aged 75 and older who had no contact with friends had an increased mortality risk—whereas women who had no contact with relatives (other than children) but did with friends did not have an increased risk of mortality. One explanation provided by the researchers for this finding was that friends were geographically closer than relatives and were better able to provide social support. In addition, the nature of the relationships, expectations, and interactions between the study subjects and their friends were most likely different than those between the subjects and their families.

The study also found that attending group organizations was associated with reduced risk of mortality only among women aged 75 or older (Yasuda et al. 2007, p. 522). This may be due to the fact that with increased age women are less likely or able to travel or participate in many activities available to younger older women, and thus contact with family, friends, and social groups may take on more value and importance as women continue to age. It was also suggested in the study that women who lived 10 years or fewer in a community may not experience the benefits of increased social contact. Being familiar with the neighborhood—its facilities, merchants, and inhabitants—could be important contributors to lowering mortality risk among elderly women.

According to a 10-year study in Australia, older people with a large group of friends "were 22% less likely to die during the study period than those with fewer friends." In 2008, "Harvard researchers reported that strong social ties could promote brain health" as people age (Parker-Pope 2009). Strong friendships have a tremendous positive effect on health and well-being.

19

Improved Physical and Emotional Functioning

Medical researchers have been examining the link between social support and physical health for the past 30 years. Cassel (1976) and Cobb (1976) demonstrated clear associations between the two in their seminal reviews, and hundreds of studies subsequently followed that further illuminated the link between social support and physical and emotional functioning (Sarason, Pierce, and Sarason 1990). One such study reports that "When individuals perceive adequate social support, the resulting goals of improved health are more likely to be achieved" (Berkman et al. 2000). The literature shows that social support helps increase psychological well-being and lowers the probability of physical illness (Cohen and Wells 1985; Wallston et al. 1983).

Being Alone Takes Its Toll

Older women are frequently susceptible to loneliness because they generally live longer than their spouses, thus experiencing more years of living alone—with much of that time in a state of increasingly declining health. Support systems may be difficult to come by. Often, older women suffer social exclusion because of gender, age, race, ethnicity, ability, and socioeconomic status (WHO 2007, p. 36). As a result of this exclusion—which may be based on barriers to education, work, citizenship, and health care—older minority women may suffer from poor health.

Socialization Needed from Many Sources

To adequately tackle the myriad issues involved with an aging population, many organizations and groups must come together and pool their resources. The health sector is equipped to address women's physical issues, whereas faith-based organizations may serve their spiritual/religious needs. Research on older women's needs from academics may offer solutions to yet another aspect of the challenges facing older women. Furthermore, organizations involved in economics, labor, housing, transportation, and civics all need to identify and provide adequate services and support to older people—and older women in particular.

An underlying theme for each of the previously cited sectors of society should be how to best keep older women involved, viable, and continuing contributors to society. To be successful, the support must occur not only on a local level but on regional, national, and international levels. To help older women feel a sense of connection with their communities and society in general, the sense of community must first be vibrant and strong in these communities.

We know from research preformed by Harvard University sociologists Christakis and Fowler that social networks influence other social networks in a community without being directly connected to those networks. For example, if out of 20 different social networks in a community only 15 elicit a feeling of life satisfaction and happiness it can be said that those 15 groups raise the overall community's life satisfaction and happiness scale through the "contagion effect." By being in the same community, but not necessarily having direct interaction with each other, social networks can and do affect each other (Christakis and Fowler 2009).

Barriers to Be Surmounted

Increasingly, social disorganization and a loss of sense of community have compromised the very fiber of previous trusting networks and the common values that grew from individuals being and feeling connected. Although this trend is affecting all demographics of individuals, a loss of community is especially relevant and detrimental to older women.

There are several possible reasons for the decline in a locality's sense of community. Pressures of time and money, including the special pressures on dual-career families, have contributed to the loss of social and community involvement. When people are busy supporting themselves and their families, they often have little time to spend on other social pursuits. Sub-urbanization, commuting, and suburban sprawl also add to the loss of community connectedness (Putnam 2001). These conditions keep people separated and socially segregated from one another. Time spent traveling to and from work, for example, takes time away from being with family and neighbors and from participating in locally organized events.

The impact of electronic communication and entertainment has had a powerful influence on the breakdown of a community's social vibrancy.

Individuals have become more passive and private with their leisure time, essentially cutting them off from other forms of social and community participation.

Perhaps the most significant influence in the diminishing sense of community is generational change. Much of the decline of community in America during the last part of the twentieth century is due to the replacement of a very civically active and highly participatory generation born between 1910 and 1940 with several other generations less involved in community life (Putnam 2001). The children and grandchildren of the more community-minded generation are part of a larger societal shift toward individual and material values, and they are being drawn away from communal values. This factor is the one with the most impact on community decline.

Older women can also be affected by the contagion effect when other social networks in their community dismiss them. These women begin to believe that they are unimportant, forgotten, not valued, and in fact don't exist in the minds of others in the community. This needs to change. However, there is hope. A sense of community can be regained by increasing social capital with one another, which benefits all generations and all members of the community—but all have to be willing participants. The benefits of social interaction are far reaching and are becoming an increasingly valuable commodity.

Support groups in particular are one forum for establishing community and connection. Participation in social support groups is a powerful tool that can help boost participants' resilience as they face challenging and changing life situations. Trust in the Lives of Older Women groups, described in more detail in Chapter 3, are designed to create a social support structure for older women who are experiencing a loss of their social networks through geographic relocation and death of family and friends.

3

BENEFITS OF SUPPORT GROUPS:

trust
in the lives
of older
women

"Trust is a basic ingredient in a healthy personality. Trust is learned early in life from mother's love (parent's love). Trust learned early in life is how a person sees himself/herself later in life."

—E. Erikson, developmental psychologist

ﹰﹰﹰﹰ ﹰﹰﹰﹰ ﹰﹰﹰﹰ ﹰﹰﹰﹰ ﹰ ﹰﹰﹰﹰ ﹰﹰﹰﹰ ﹰﹰﹰﹰ ﹰﹰﹰﹰ

Social support for older women can take many forms—from informal connection with family and friends to structured time with other women, through support groups or activities based on common interests (e.g., knitting clubs) or religious affiliation. "Older women may feel that their families give them support out of a sense of duty, while friends do so with the expectation that each can contribute to the other's welfare by helping out on an equal basis" (Unger and Crawford 1992, p. 526).

One example of social connection and camaraderie is the support group. Support groups provide a forum for women to share their experiences with other women and provide a valuable resource to help them through difficult times such as serious illness, bereavement, challenging periods of transition, and adjustment to the aging process. Support groups are a safe place for older women to talk about what distresses them and to explore ways to reduce their challenges.

Diverse cultures have different philosophies and methods of dealing with their older population, and being part of a support group can help protect women and give them a voice with which to stand up for their rights and their value. Social interaction and involvement with others also helps the older women specifically, and the community in general, to address the social exclusion of widows and the infringement on their human rights (WHO 2007, p. 39).

According to the article "Women, Ageing [*sic*] and Health: A Framework for Action," published by the World Health Organization (45), more effort must be placed on,

...establishing or strengthening programmes [sic], policies, services and research efforts that promote mental health and manage mental illnesses that affect older people. For many women, it is especially important to increase awareness about and reduce the stigma associated with depression; to protect the rights and dignity of older people with Alzheimer [sic] disease and other forms of dementia; to reduce gender-based stereotyping related to menopause and the use of psychotropic drugs; and to support the mental health of older people who have experienced elder abuse or other forms of violence at any stage of their lives.

Additional topics relevant to older women that could be the focus of support groups include their treatment and coverage by the media, accurate reporting of the levels of elder abuse and domestic violence as experienced by this population, and determining how to best address physical and emotional abuse against them.

A priority issue for many support groups is to try to improve the economic, social, and physical well-being of their members. Such groups also strive to socially include all aging women, with an emphasis on reaching out to older women who have become isolated. To help accomplish this objective, supporting organizations create environments that enable women to become physically and socially involved in community life. Providing a safe and reassuring venue also strengthens the older woman's sense of empowerment, thus encouraging her to share capabilities and experiences and to explore new avenues of activity, freedom of movement, and self-fulfillment. Support groups are vital to the well-being of older women and may be a critical factor in fostering their resilience.

Trust in the Lives of Older Women

Trust in the Lives of Older Women (TLOW) groups are designed to address the specific concerns and challenges faced by older women. The uniqueness of this approach is that TLOW groups augment already established programs for older women. Neither disease- nor issue-focused, this concept provides a positive and ongoing support structure based on trust for older women. Women can share their life experiences, increase their self-confidence, and build lasting relationships.

Support from the community gives women an opportunity to share the intuitive wisdom of their hearts as they create safe places for building relationships. Participants obtain ongoing support that helps them through a variety of life challenges—such as the loss of a spouse, of family members, and of friends; living alone; and continuing to act as caregivers to spouses, grandchildren, and even friends. As a result, older women are able to stay in the community instead of having to move away (i.e., to live with their children).

Women stay healthier longer by participating in groups and by making valuable contributions to the community. They become more independent and make less of a demand on the health care system in their community. TLOW groups provide a social network for older women, from which they, their families, and their communities benefit. Members of groups enjoy a boost in their resilience and an increase in their overall life satisfaction.

A study by Christakis and Fowler (2009, p. 56) found that a person is 45% more likely to be happy if a friend became happy in the previous six months. This supports the fact that TLOW group members can and do have an effect on one another.

Trust Defined

Webster's dictionary defines trust as a reliance on the integrity, ability, or character of a person or thing. Trust is a two-way street. It is reaching out and communicating to others and receiving others as they reach out in return.

Elements of Trust

There are three primary elements in establishing trust in TLOW groups: Trust formation, meeting basic needs, and creating a psychological sense of community.

Trust Formation

Trust formation develops in a group or community when:

- ❖ Acceptance is present
- ❖ Feedback is established (communicate back and forth)

❖ Goals are created
❖ Personal control and self-management are practiced

Ron Hofsess has adapted and applied Jack Gibb's work in trust formation to the TLOW method and proposes that the development of trust is enhanced in the following ways:

❖ Reaching out to others
❖ Sharing personal information
❖ Reducing fears with one another (creating safe places)
❖ Making and keeping agreements
❖ Communicating with one another
❖ Cooperating with one another
❖ Taking risks with one another
❖ Reducing constraints/expectations/controls
❖ Reducing role-defined views of ourselves

For example, taking a risk with someone by letting him or her know something about you that most people don't know is a leap toward showing trust. It is a way of creating a trust relationship. It is saying to the person, "I think you are trustworthy enough to know this about me." This risk-taking, trusting behavior often results in reciprocation of sharing personal information—which leads to deeper connection.

High-trust relationships, such as best friends, are characterized by safety to share experiences and risk taking. High-trust relationships are facilitated in trust groups. For example, after the group has been established for several months the members are asked about a time they were betrayed in their lives. Sharing this betrayal of trust in a previous relationship demonstrates trust formation in the TLOW groups because the women are willing to be vulnerable with one another about a life experience.

Meeting Basic Needs

The second element in forming a TLOW group is meeting basic needs. William Glasser's "choice theory" (1998) has been used as one of the three principles underlying the TLOW groups. Choice theory postulates that all behavior is purposeful: either we behave in a way that somehow meets our need for a more quality world, or we don't. Glasser identifies basic human needs as survival, power/achievement, fun, freedom, love, and belonging. TLOW groups allow group members to identify and meet these needs.

Although people share the same basic human needs, they differ in the amount of each need required. For example, whereas some people have a high need for social connections (love and belonging) others are more driven by the need to achieve (power), the need to play (fun), the need for independence (freedom), or the need to be healthy and/or financially secure (survival). Glasser's theory includes psychological and physical needs.

Psychological Needs:

- ❖ *Love/belonging:* friendship, caring, involvement
- ❖ *Fun:* play, enjoyment, laughter, pleasure
- ❖ *Power:* achievement, recognition, competence, skill
- ❖ *Freedom:* autonomy, choice, independence

Physical Needs:

- ❖ *Survival*
- ❖ *Food*
- ❖ *Clothing*
- ❖ *Shelter*

Meeting basic needs in the TLOW group is always a focus. This is seen in the two-hour group meeting design. In the first hour, group members are asked to share what is going on in their lives and how specific needs are being met. In the second hour, the group discusses a topic of interest all have in common— one that encourages meeting the group members' needs.

Creating a Psychological Sense of Community

The third element of a TLOW group is the creation of a psychological sense of community. A sense of community is achieved when members experience the following: they feel that they belong, have a shared faith that their needs will be met, matter to one another, and have a commitment to be together (McMillan and Chavis 1986). The following are key ingredients in creating a psychological sense of community.

- ❖ An agreed-upon purpose for being together
- ❖ Meeting one another's needs as group members
- ❖ Shared leadership
- ❖ Creating a safe place for individuals to take risks and be vulnerable
- ❖ Free flow of communication among group members
- ❖ Authority figures giving up their assumed roles and their status symbols
- ❖ Group members' need for solitude
- ❖ Recognizing that the community is essential for human needs

A psychological sense of community is created in TLOW groups in a variety of ways. The group members agree upon ways they want to be together individually and collectively. They pay attention to one another's needs in the group meetings and outside the group. They call or visit one another—especially if members haven't been to the group meeting in awhile. They often share group leadership through the discussion of various topics of interest.

The Structure of TLOW Groups

Facilitators are trained in these three models: trust formation, meeting basic needs, and creating a psychological sense of community. They are encouraged to pay attention to facilitating within their groups the ideas and concepts behind these models. TLOW groups begin as trained facilitators lead participants through four start-up sessions. In these sessions, facilitators share with participants the TLOW model based on the trust concepts previously discussed—as well as the process and procedures for implementing the model. Participants learn that their TLOW group is all about them.

In the first hour of the group meeting, the women share as much or as little as they like about what has happened in their lives during the past week. In the second hour, they discuss a topic of group interest based on the needs of the group members (e.g., health issues in a woman's later years, home safety, forgiveness and reconciliation, or staying positive during life transitions). See Appendix D for a list of the topics covered in TLOW groups. At the conclusion of the four start-up sessions, participants decide if they want to continue meeting on a weekly or other regular basis. TLOW groups have been established in any setting where older women gather, such as senior centers, churches, retirement living centers, and college alumni meetings.

Facilitators can be social workers, teachers, nurses, or anyone working with older women. Facilitators often have similar yet varied characteristics—most notably all having caring qualities, sensitivity, and the desire to work with older women. Facilitators learn about key elements in creating communities of trust, understand the value of these groups, and learn the process for starting these groups. Suitable characteristics of facilitators can be determined by referring to Appendix C for the trust group facilitator assessment.

TLOW groups provide many benefits. Participants report decreased stress, loneliness, and anxiety—as well as increased support, friendship, laughter, and mental stimulation. By encouraging participants to share experiences and challenges related to their current life situations, TLOW groups serve to boost participants' resilience. The families of participants and their communities also benefit, as participants in these groups increase their ability to remain independent in their homes, use fewer critical resources in their communities, and experience decreased "burnout" as caregivers.

4

THE VOICES OF OLDER WOMEN AND SUPPORTERS

trust in the lives of older women

"It is well to be good to women in the strength of our manhood because we must sit under their hands at both ends of our lives."

—He Dog, Oglala Lakota

�ᛉ ᛉᛉᛉ ᛚᛉᛉᛉ ᛟ ᛉᛉᛉᛉ ᛉᛉᛉᛉ ᛉᛉᛉᛉ

There has been growing support for the program Trust in the Lives of Older Women (TLOW). TLOW groups are supported by a U.S. Congressional resolution.

Congressional Resolution

The following is taken from U.S. Congressional Resolution 855, submitted by Congressman Amo Houghton in November of 2004.

Resolved that the House of Representatives;

1. *Recognizes that the Trust in the Lives of Older Women program benefits older women by decreasing their stress, isolation, anxiety, and depression and providing trust, support, friendship, community, and mental stimulation;*
2. *Commends the Trust in the Lives of Older Women program for encouraging older women to stay healthy and to continue making contributions to their communities, and*
3. *Encourages community groups, including religious organizations, colleges and universities, and community centers to participate in the program by starting groups in their communities.*

Comments from Supporters of the TLOW Program

The following are comments from individuals and agencies with a vested interest in support programs such as TLOW.

❖ Attendees, International Federation on Aging Conference in Singapore, September of 2004

Bring Trust in the Lives of Older Women group facilitator training to the region.

❖ U.S. Administration on Aging (AoA), November of 2004, eNews

The Trust in the Lives of Older Women program shows great promise in helping individuals deal with the multitude of aging problems... preliminary studies suggest members experience beneficial health effects, better attitudes toward aging, and increased volunteerism.

❖ Christy Balliett, Director of the Corning Senior Center, Corning, New York, January of 2002

The women [in the Trust in the Lives of Older Women groups] have actually blossomed and opened up right in front of our eyes. They have reached out to each other and have formed strong bonds, not only inside the group but outside as well.

❖ Larry Wilson, feature writer, *Star Gazette*, Elmira, New York, October 12, 2004

A support group for older women may soon be in use throughout the United States and in other nations.

❖ Robert Dunphy, Director of the Schuyler County (New York) Office of the Aging, July of 2004

[Trust in the Lives of Older Women] groups have beneficial effects on health, mentally and physically...women who participate in the programs have better attitudes toward aging...I think [the program] has application not just in the Southern Tier of New York but throughout the nation.

Comments from Members of TLOW Groups

❖ *My life has completely changed since joining the Trust Group for Older Women. Thanks! Ron.*

❖ *Belonging! Being trusted and listened to. Always knowing that I will never be judged. I can just be myself. A wonderful group of new friends. Thank you!*

❖ *Joining Trust in the Lives of Older Women was one of the best things that I have done in my life. I have made many friends, had lots of fun and am so glad Ron started the group.*

❖ *I have enjoyed the fellowship this group has brought me.*

❖ *Participating in the Trust group has added a new richness and dimension to my life. It has added to my growth!*

❖ *Ron, you are doing extremely important work.*

❖ *Ron, I really enjoy the "Trust group" and watching the group grow.*

❖ *This group has added a new interest and dimension to my life: renewed old friendships and created new ones. It is definitely a worthwhile activity for older women, especially those who are living alone.*

❖ *Ron, I joined this group for six years, and I know that you and this group helped me when I was terribly disturbed about my sister's illness and etc. You and this group and the college group helped me. Amen!!*

❖ *For me it is sheer joy to join this group. I learned a great deal and made new friends. I experience love like the love of a family...among the group, attitudes have changed since we have gotten together. Attitude is very important. A good attitude is what makes one's life beautiful...and I feel that my life has been made more beautiful by being a member of this group.*

❖ *When I reached an "older age" I knew what many women meant when they said "no one sees an old woman." "Old women are invisible." I found that to be true. It seems to me that I was invisible and began feeling diminished in many ways. Then I was invited to an Older Women's Trust Group. The women listened, cared, supported me by validating my thoughts, ideas and contributions to the group. By sharing feelings and happenings and laughter week after week my attitudes have changed, my spirit has returned. I know I've grown–am more open–and know older women are not invisible.*

❖ *Renewed old friendships. Made new ones. Was listened to in the group and given support.*

❖ *I foresee this will spread around the world one day.*

Comments from a Typical Local TLOW Group

The following are comments from the Trust in the Lives of Older Women group that now meets at a local church. Upon reading these comments, I'm sure you will readily understand my joy and fulfillment as being their group facilitator! I am blessed!

❖ *I've been with the group for two years, I've gotten a lot of knowledge, I've met many lovely friends; I really enjoy our sharing!!*

❖ *I was an original member of the college group and was pleased to meet ACTIVE older women who can contribute so much to our community. "The last of life for which first is made": so true.*

❖ *I have been in the Trust group for two years. I have met women with different social backgrounds. We come together to help each other when there are trials and tribulations in our lives.*

❖ *I'm a five-year member. We support one another by listening, encouraging, and advising each other. We plan programs that meet our needs and enrich our lives.*

❖ *I joined the group about six years ago. It's been an interesting journey with an active, fun group of newly formed friends.*

❖ *My experience with "Trust in the Lives of Older Women" has been one of sharing and caring. I've been a member since 2001 and though there have been health and travel issues that have prevented me from attending regularly, I've always felt accepted and respected. The women of the group provide a network of friendship that I consider a blessing in my life.*

❖ *In 1990 I joined the trust group made up mostly of my college alumni under the direction of Dr. Ron Hofsess. The women of the group warmly accepted each other and shared their knowledge and varied experiences. We learned so much from each other and totally supported one another through illnesses or the death of a loved one. We also shared our joys and loved to celebrate special occasions together. Although the group has changed from time to time, there is still a great spirit of caring and trust. I've thoroughly enjoyed being a member.*

❖ *I feel very fortunate to be a member of our Trust group (Trust in the Lives of Older Women). Every woman in my group I consider a very close friend. The friendships are the most important aspect of the group for me. The activities that we plan, be it speakers, crafts, luncheons, book reports, health insurance and many others are always stimulating and fun. It is a very relaxed atmosphere and I know that I feel very comfortable sharing anything with my "trust" friends.*

❖ *I learn so much every week (when I attend meetings) about so many subjects. I'm always energized by the enthusiasm for life and living, from hearing about interesting and important books. The laughter and fun are just wonderful!*

❖ *I enjoy the friendship, caring and support of my group.*

❖ *I enjoy being a part of a group of folks I don't see in other areas of my life. It's nice to know new people.*

❖ *My interest in Trust in the Lives of Older Women began about two years ago when an article appeared in the local newspaper with a picture featuring the coordinators of local groups. Since Ann, the coordinator of the group which now meets at a local church, has been a friend for many years, I decided to investigate. My initial meeting and introduction to other members of the group has led me to become an active part of the friendship, fellowship and fun I have come to look forward to every second and fourth Tuesday. We share our lives, past and present, we join others in presenting our experience and expertise in all areas and interests; we look to each other for affirmation and encouragement; and in doing these things, we've formed a bond which enriches our lives.*

❖ *My "Trust among older women" group emphasizes the importance of reaching out to others by listening to their current problems and helping with their future plans.*

❖ *It's a very, very interesting group. It's such an awakening since I was so used to caring for elderly people who were not well and then, to be with a group where these people in their later years, like me too, are vibrant and lively. The one thing that I liked about this group at the beginning was that it was such a personal group. It wasn't that you had to join the group and do something, like a service organization. We had programs, did projects together, and went on field trips and luncheons. It was really a lot of fun. I think some of our best meetings have been when we haven't had an agenda and we just had something to talk about that included everybody. It made you feel closer to the people; you got to know them better. I think everybody felt very comfortable with each other. The trust part was the main thing. It was the sort of group that you knew you could say anything that you wanted to and it would go no farther than that room.*

5

ENVISIONING
THE FUTURE

trust in the lives
of older women

*"We must act as elders of the tribe, looking out for the best interests
of the future and preserving the precious compact between generations."*

**—Maggie Kuhn, American civic activist and founder
of the Grey Panthers**

Most of the current research involving gerontologic and women's studies has failed to address the problems of aging women (United Nations 1995b). To fill this void in information, organizations on all levels—including governments, the public and non-profit sectors, and academia—need to join forces and share resources to institute a plan to promote research on the relationship between poverty, aging, and gender. All research and studies related to the situation of aging women must be analyzed and integrated to formulate a broad overview of the older woman's plight.

The Role of Researchers

When designing research studies and methods of obtaining data, researchers must incorporate the older woman's voice as well as her overall condition. Qualitative methodology may prove an effective research strategy for highlighting the themes in the minimally documented older women's experience. Recording oral histories could prove very helpful in providing a record of the contributions older women make to society.

The Role of Government

Governments have an obligation to protect their most vulnerable citizens, and older women too often fit that category. Governments could do many things to improve the older woman's situation. Policies could be designed and implemented to strengthen and make more efficient existing minimal income and social safety nets for all older people in need, not just women. Laws could be amended so that women are no longer discriminated against in the case of

43

property and inheritance rights. Property taxes on residences of older people could be eliminated.

The Role of Health Care Providers

Health care providers should be educated to better recognize the unique health issues of aging women, and trained to treat them accordingly. Mental health services that are better focused to treat women's diverse backgrounds and life issues could be made available. To encourage and maintain independence, governments could provide aging and physically challenged older women with homecare services and other healthcare-related assistance. The locally implemented cost-efficient benefits of TLOW groups accrue over time and help minimize the costly burden borne by state and federal assistance programs.

TLOW Benefits to Older Individuals

TLOW groups provide a social support structure for older women as a partial replacement for the loss of community women face because they outlive so many among their family and friends. These groups also create a safe place for building relationships and boosting participants' resilience as they face various life situations. Women participating in these groups report many benefits. Among these benefits are decreased stress, loneliness, depression, and anxiety and increased support, friendships, sense of community, humor and laughter, mental stimulation, feeling of trust, and relief from anxiety.

TLOW Benefits to the Community

Communities benefit from TLOW groups in numerous ways. Women stay in and contribute to the community longer, versus moving away to live with their children, other family member, or some other person. Women also draw less on the health care system and continue to make contributions to their communities while remaining independent in their homes. It is important to note that the start-up and maintenance costs associated with TLOW groups are low. For Example:

❖ The cost of training a group facilitator is no more than $400.

❖ Meeting places are typically provided for free or by a sponsor, or charged at a nominal fee.

❖ Participation is free to individuals.

The Community Role

There are many things that can be done to help the older woman age with grace, dignity, and greater independence. Forming a social support structure in a community is a huge asset in the lives of older women. Helping older women find new ways to participate in society and their community enriches their lives with a renewed sense of purpose and involvement, enabling them to not only share the wealth of their experiences but to learn new skills and keep current with technology, methods of communication, and their local environment.

The Role of NGOs

A long-held goal of non-governmental organizations (NGOs) has been to convince the U.N. body, the Committee on the Elimination of all forms of Discrimination Against Women (CEDAW), to "include older women as a category for examining unequal treatment" (Global Action on Aging, November 17, 2008). In a report from the World Health Organization titled "Women, Ageing and Health: A Framework for Action," many suggestions are offered that would help ease the hardship of older women as a result of poverty—particularly in their later years. The following is a summary of these suggestions.

❖ Caregivers of family members who are ill or frail should be supported to ease the financial burden and loss of employment that often results from taking on this role.

❖ Women still in the labor market should be allowed greater flexibility in their work practice to enable them to continue their caregiver role.

❖ Older women should be encouraged to save for retirement and long-term care needs.

45

❖ Health care should be ensured and easily accessible.

❖ All inheritance rights should be upheld when a parent or spouse dies.

❖ All older women should have an income that allows them to provide the basic necessities of life.

❖ Additional support should be made available to older women who live alone, are widowed, are poor or disabled, or who require long-term care either in their own home or in an assisted-living location.

❖ If required, support should be provided for compassionate end-of-life care and appropriate burial arrangements.

Some progress is being made in the effort to provide better and more support for older women as they age, but so much more needs to be done.

The Larger Mission

Older women provide a tremendously vital element to the well-being of all with whom they come into contact. They are the primary caregivers for so many for so long; their contributions and sacrifices should not go unnoticed. Older women deserve to be supported and encouraged to maintain their independence, to be given ample opportunities to participate in community activities, and to be provided with adequate and appropriate care. They deserve to live their lives fully and with dignity. It is imperative that we better understand how the aging process affects the social, personal, physical, emotional, and economic elements of their lives.

Once society as a whole grasps the needs of older women and comes to value the contribution older women make to everyone's lives, many misconceptions and myths about women and aging will be debunked. With better policies and programs in place to more effectively support this group, perhaps the words "older women" will be seen as a celebration of life.

Communities in particular can help in the effort to educate, understand, and appreciate older women. As a member of your community, contact Choose 2 Trust—which has initiated the TLOW program discussed in this book—for information on starting a support group and spreading the celebration of life.

6

REFLECTIONS
AND
RESPONSES

"So much has been said and written about men, why don't we wake up to the contribution of older women?"

—Ron Hofsess, adult educator

In writing this book, I am in no way implying that only negative events happen to older women—nor am I saying that no positive treatment exists in the world for older women. I am pointing out that there is a need to provide more resources and assistance to older women because they need it (more so as major caregivers to their families, communities, and society) and because they are deprived of their fair share for survival. There is an imbalance in the distribution of resources for older women compared to other demographic groups. During an informal interview, Ron Hofsess responded to some general questions regarding the topics covered in this book.

❖ *Was there any particular event or situation that first prompted the ideas that evolved into the Trust in the Lives of Older Women program?*

I can't think of a specific event, it was an evolution of my different life experiences. I grew up in a family where my parents could have easily been my grandparents. When I was born and I already had nieces and nephews, my sisters could have been my mom—and the friends of my parents were older and they were around the house. So, as I was growing up I was around a lot of older people—not thinking anything differently about it. I do remember my mother would have church circles over to the house.

I remember one was called the Priscilla Circle, and older women would come and meet and talk. Also, my folks tended to a family down the street; my father would help them. The woman was quite incapacitated and they were very good friends of my family and I would go over and visit with them quite often and watch baseball games with the man. That was an early underpinning of influence I think.

Right now I have three sisters in their eighties and they're still alive, so I think that early experience probably shaped something in my awareness and helped me on the path toward this idea. And I think my background in human services and sociology and psychology and gerontology, and being in the Peace Corps, all contributed to the sensitivity to work with social issues and those experiences knit and wove a fabric that brought me to look at this idea.

❖ *When you were younger did you ever notice if older people were treated differently than, say, your parents or other adults?*

I remember having good associations with my folks' friends and didn't think much of it, discerning the treatment toward older people. I didn't notice anything that put them in a lesser status until I got older.

❖ *When you got older and saw more of the world and how people in general are treated, did you pick up any changes in the treatment of older people?*

When I got into college and my studies in sociology and anthropology and looking at other cultures, reading about certain demographics and older women in particular, I saw how they were often treated as chattel. That raised my sensitivity. My Peace Corps experience in Iran also heightened my awareness. I lived in Iran for two years. I saw poverty in a way that I never imagined as a young man at that time. It was like looking through a new lens on the world. When I came back to the United States, I began to notice how older people were treated—particularly older women.

❖ *What do you find most rewarding about your involvement with the TLOW program?*

What I find most rewarding is just enjoying being in the different groups for a number of reasons. One is what happens when the women talk about what is going on in their lives, and how healing that is for them. Another is the depth of their life trauma and their experiences with their families and their spouses and the personal in-depth sharing. We don't often have many safe places in our lives to do that and this is a place that allows that to happen.

The surprising piece for me is that when I first started these groups I thought that I'd be offering something to these women to help them in their own life adjustments and what I found was I got far more from it because of what I call the intuitive wisdom of the hearts in these women—just sharing, almost instinctively, what's going on with them and how supportive they are. This is especially true for those in the group that came through some of the life transitions that other women are just now approaching, like losing a spouse.

I don't find going to these groups as a dutiful thing to do; I enjoy going to them whenever I can. I get as much out of these groups as they do, and I hadn't thought about it like that when I first started. And the facilitators reference that as well for themselves. Everybody wins. These groups are created and steeped in a trusting environment and that's the core, the key ingredient. There's an agreement that this is a trusting, safe place, and that opens up the members to feel safe to talk about what's going on with them. When they share the richness of their lives, then that just adds to it. They have a forum or stage from which to share their stories and it's important that it's a safe place.

❖ *What is the biggest obstacle you've encountered that has hampered your research on the topic of older women?*

A significant piece is the lack of research available in looking at this demographic of older women. There isn't very much and I'm finding out that few studies have been done on this population. I'm getting as much from my own application and training in terms of the value and the importance of this kind of learning opportunity (for example, starting TLOW groups) as I am almost from the research. However, the research does document the marginalization of older women.

Plus, getting financial assistance is a real barrier. People I talk with love the idea and say, go do it, but trying to get assistance is hard. So, lack of research and lack of resources are probably my biggest obstacles—which is very much representative of the pattern of what this population has to deal with, not having resources to support their life circumstances. Often, in some studies just done on men, researchers would just extrapolate and project how it would affect women.

❖ *Have you personally seen in society how older women are being marginalized?*

Oh yes, I think so. When I was in the Middle East I saw that very clearly, both in how they were treated as well as the lack of resources that were available to them. How they were treated in terms of being controlled, how their role was defined by society, and the man being in charge. They often lived in extreme poverty. Even men who are in poverty situations have more freedom and more resources than the women. You'll see older men who very clearly are not from a wealthy class and they are just hanging out with other men, smoking their pipes and engaging with each other. They're out having some coffee and that costs money—but you don't see women engaging in public in that manner.

❖ *How about on a domestic level, and the dealings with the women in your program?*

Yes, with the different groups that we have there's a range of economic backgrounds (for example, a college alumni group). I would say that they're not necessarily well-to-do, but they are not struggling along in getting resources—but even within that group there are some who are just getting by. And especially with some of the other groups, they're more from a lower socioeconomic class, blue-collar setting, and some will say, "Well, if we're going to go out to lunch, I can't afford to do that," and the others will chip in and help the person to join them.

❖ *So do you think economics has a direct impact on how women are treated or seen in society? Do you think society looks at them differently if they're not necessarily well dressed or look like they're from a more comfortable social or economic class?*

Oh, I think exactly that. There's a gender and class stereotype and you can see the difference in how they are treated.

❖ *What's the most disturbing issue you've experienced that has the most negative effect on older women?*

Clearly the loss of the spouse has a negative effect on the women, especially if they've been married for a long time. The most disturbing piece of that to me is if the spouse abused her. For example, she may have chosen to stay in the relationship for decades and saw some good in the relationship and in her husband—but also had to endure physical and psychological abuse. I've heard a number of stories where that's true. I found that very unsettling.

I can remember one woman sharing her story of abuse and it brought her to tears remembering it, and as I looked around at the other women in attendance they were nodding their heads and showing some real emotion as well—not only empathy toward the woman sharing it but likely recalling some of their own experience with abuse by their husbands. So that was one of the more disturbing things for me to see.

❖ *Women often feel trapped in relationships and feel they have nowhere else to go, no support system to turn to, so they stay in an unhealthy relationship.*

That's very true, and their loyalty to the relationship and the marriage keeps them sustained in it in a way that they think *Maybe it will get better, maybe things will change, let's try it again.* They see their love as so enduring that they can withstand these abuses. That's the way they were brought up. They show their enduring loyalty in spite of the abuse.

❖ *How does one foster trust in a relationship?*

That's a great question. I think all of us know, but we may not think about how we do it but we all have been able to create trust most of the time in our lives. There are a number of ways for that to happen. I think the degree to which I create fewer constraints in my relationship enhances the trust level. For example, if I have fewer expectations about what I want from that person the more trusting I am because I'm not asking that person to behave in a certain way. Also, the more spontaneous I am the more likely trust is going to get nurtured.

When I'm in a playful, spontaneous place I'm in a pretty trusting place because I'm not checking what I'm thinking or feeling. I sort of let myself show who I am. This is one of the exciting pieces about the concept of trust: it has an elasticity. There's an agreement and a predictability that you're going to do what you say and keep your word. And that means that there's a stability about keeping your agreement. On the other end, there's a spontaneity piece;

that if I can let myself also show in spontaneous ways what I'm thinking and feeling then that's an example of trust because I feel safe to not have to always think and show myself in a predictable way that's going to be acceptable to this other person. Those ingredients are important.

And trust is a two-way street. It's giving and receiving. If I'm giving from my own personal life experience, from my heart and my thoughts without checking them, I'm sharing and not holding back, and at the same time I'm also inviting that other person to do the same thing. Think about when you're with good friends, more with them than anybody, is the fact that you're not checking what you're thinking or feeling and you're just there in a spontaneous way. You just flow, and that when you're with people you don't know you're more often on guard and cautious until the relationship evolves in a more trusting way.

Taking risk is also important. I've seen in groups where people come together, never having been together before, and someone begins to share something personal. They are taking a risk, and that often opens up others. They see the similarity that they may have experienced and in turn open up and share their story and it has that ripple effect. So, taking a risk to share something personal about themselves and not just hiding behind a role-defined view of who I am (like a teacher, counselor, priest, or whatever) if I relate only in those ways then you don't get to know the more vulnerable parts of me.

❖ *Do you have any other thoughts you'd like to share that we haven't covered in any of the previous questions?*

I'm envisioning these groups getting started in any community that wants to have them and I hope that most communities would want a group like this for its older women citizens. I think that such a positive outcome takes place for everybody: the women in the group and the community. I would like to see these groups as popular as AA is around the world in terms of its contribution. I think TLOW groups have merit and hopefully we will have the support for creating more groups in more communities.

✝ APPENDIX A ⛊

Problems That Affect Older Women's Social Participation

Physical	*Social*	*Psychological*	*Economic*	*Spiritual*
Physical decline through chronic disease creates locomotor activity limitations	Isolation	Older women have high rates of depression but when treated recover quickly	Few resources	Life crises challenge one's religious beliefs, especially when living alone with no one to talk to about those problems
Osteoporosis	Living alone	Loss of self-esteem as they age	Often living at a subsistence level	
	Lower levels of social participation due to physical decline		Constant struggle to get by	
			Little time for social connections	

☥ APPENDIX B ☥

Benefits of TLOW Groups for Older Women

☥☥☥☥ ☥☥☥☥ ☥☥☥☥ ☥☥☥☥ ☥ ☥☥☥☥ ☥☥☥☥ ☥☥☥☥ ☥☥☥☥

Physical	*Social*	*Psychological*	*Economic*	*Spiritual*
Mental stimulation	Friendships that lead to informal care- giving of each other	In-depth psychological support and self-esteem through having opportunities to share with the group	Speakers come in with ideas to curb costs of daily living	Inspiration of others' coping experiences increasing spiritual sense and resilience in the face of continual life challenges
		Intimate relationships with other members	On a limited basis, participants learn from each other ways to reduce everyday expenses and help others who can't afford an activity the group has planned	

♂ APPENDIX C ♙

Trust Group Facilitator Self-assessment

♙♙♙ ♙♙♙ ♙♙♙ ♙♙♙ ♂ ♙♙♙ ♙♙♙ ♙♙♙ ♙♙♙

This is an assessment scale to help you assess your level of comfort with some of the behaviors/characteristics that have been identified as important in the facilitator role. Here you can rate your comfort level with each of the behaviors/characteristics that follow. At one end of the scale is the number 1, which represents Not at All Comfortable—and at the other end is the number 10, which represents Extremely Comfortable. When you are finished, assess the scores on an item basis. The goal is to achieve 8s and above for all items. Lower scores indicate that you might want to key in on a particular item or items and do the work necessary to raise the score. This tool can be used to help you focus on areas to improve to be able to assume the facilitator role more easily.

1. I have patience.

Not at all Comfortable   Extremely Comfortable

1   2   3   4   5   6   7   8   9   10

2. I like older women.

Not at all Comfortable   Extremely Comfortable

1   2   3   4   5   6   7   8   9   10

3. I have a diverse perspective.

Not at all Comfortable   Extremely Comfortable

1   2   3   4   5   6   7   8   9   10

4. I am optimistic.

Not at all Comfortable   Extremely Comfortable

1   2   3   4   5   6   7   8   9   10

5. I have empathy.

Not at all Comfortable   Extremely Comfortable

1   2   3   4   5   6   7   8   9   10

6. I am friendly.

Not at all Comfortable   Extremely Comfortable

1   2   3   4   5   6   7   8   9   10

7. I mediate.

Not at all Comfortable   Extremely Comfortable

1   2   3   4   5   6   7   8   9   10

8. I communicate.

Not at all Comfortable   Extremely Comfortable

1   2   3   4   5   6   7   8   9   10

9. I am open-minded.

Not at all Comfortable   Extremely Comfortable

1   2   3   4   5   6   7   8   9   10

10. I listen.

Not at all Comfortable   Extremely Comfortable

1   2   3   4   5   6   7   8   9   10

11. I summarize.

Not at all Comfortable   Extremely Comfortable

1   2   3   4   5   6   7   8   9   10

12. I time-keep.

Not at all Comfortable   Extremely Comfortable

1   2   3   4   5   6   7   8   9   10

13. I do detail work.

Not at all Comfortable   Extremely Comfortable

1   2   3   4   5   6   7   8   9   10

14. I keep the group moving.

Not at all Comfortable   Extremely Comfortable

1   2   3   4   5   6   7   8   9   10

Appendix D

Topics Selected and Used by TLOW Groups

Acceptance of Life: Being Satisfied Where We Are

Adjusting to Aging; Planning Ahead for Life Changes

Anger Management

Breathwork

Caring for Ourselves

Celebrating and Honoring Our Mothers

Choice Theory

Container Gardening

Creating a Trust Group Scrapbook

Creating Trust

Creating Trust and Spontaneity in Your Life

Current Events

Dealing with Change (cultural, family values, etc.)

Dealing with Conflict

Depression

Developing a Positive Attitude

Developing New Relationships

Discerning Trust in People Around You

Dreams

Dreams and Dreaming

Elmira Trolley and Lunch

Embracing the Millennium

Enhancing Your Memory

Exercise for Seniors

Family Photos

Favorite Quotations

Finances: Who Do You Trust?

Flower Arranging

Forgiveness

Forgiveness and Reconciliation

Funeral Planning

Get Up on Your Soapbox: Issues of Importance to You

Giving Thanks Celebration

Grand-parenting

Grief and Loss

Handling Stress

Healing and Prayers

Health Care Proxy

Healthy Living

Herbal Dreams

Hobbies and Life Passions

Holiday Sing-a-Long

Hot Flashes Journal

How the Holidays Affect Us

How to Be Vulnerable Without Being Victimized

Hugging for Health

Increasing Life Satisfaction

International Cuisine

Interviewing Others About Their Life Condition

Journal Work

Joy and Humor

Laughing Matters

Laughter: The Health Benefits

Letting Go of the Past

Life Goals: Don't Die with the Music Inside

Life on the Other Side

Lunch at Castel Grisch

Lunch on the Keuka Maid

Make-up for the Older Woman

Massage Therapy

Musicology

Musicology and Meditation

My One Moment of Fame

New Year's Resolutions: Nutrition and Dieting

Our Memories: Our Families

Parenting: Raising Our Children to Become The Best

Pets: Humorous Stories and Comforting Love

Poetry Reading

Preparing or Changing a Will

Psychic Ted Silverhand

Reaching Out

Reflexology

Reflexology: Learning What Our Feet Tell Us

Reiki

Reinventing Our Lives

Relaxation and Breathing

Saturday Morning Breakfast with Elmira Group

Seminar: Protecting Your Assets

Sharing Favorite Readings (poems, book passages, etc.)

Sharing Hobbies/Interests

Sharing Things About Yourself

Shoulda, Coulda, Woulda

Simplifying Your Life

Skin and Hair Care

Spiritual Healing and Readings

Spirituality

Stress Management in the Older Years

Summer Picnic

Tai Chi

The Art of Being Nonjudgmental

The Joys of Old Age

Thoughts for the New Year

Trusting Our Children

Types of Love

Ways to Deal with Controlling People

Wellness

What Makes a Person Lose Trust, and How to Regain It

Wisdom and Successful Aging

Writing Our Own Obituary/Eulogy

† APPENDIX E 👥

Contributions of Older Women

👥👥👥👥 † 👥👥👥👥

Older women have made many contributions in their later years. The following are examples of some of those contributions. *The following excerpts were obtained from the pamphlet "Did You Know," reprinted with permission of author Gene D. Cohen, M.D., Ph.D., and publisher Quill, an imprint of HarperCollins Publishers.*

Ethel Percy Andrus

In 1956, at age 72, Ethel Percy Andrus (1884 – 1967) was the primary force behind the establishment of the nation's first health insurance plan for people over age 65. Her advocacy efforts resulted in low-cost insurance for members of the National Retired Teachers Association. In 1958, at age 74, she founded and became president of the American Association of Retired Persons (AARP).

Emily Green Balch

Emily Green Balch (1867 – 1961) was an American political scientist, socialist, economist, social reformer, and pacifist. She was a leader of the women's movement for peace during World War I. She helped establish the Women's International League for Peace and Freedom in 1919 (at age 52), and was the group's secretary-treasurer from 1934 to 1935 (at ages 67 and 68). She continued promoting peace throughout her lifetime, sharing the Nobel Peace Prize in 1946 (at age 79) with John Raleigh Mott (age 81) and writing *Toward Human Unity* in 1952 (at age 85).

Sarah Bernhardt

Sarah Bernhardt (1844 – 1923) was the celebrated French actress who became one of the best-known performers in the history of the stage. She made her debut in 1862, achieving fame by age 25 in the role of Zanetto in Coppe's *La Passant*. In 1915, at age 71, she had to have a leg amputated following complications from an earlier knee injury received when jumping during the last scene of *La Tosca*. Nonetheless, her acting continued as playwrights found or developed roles for her that could be acted while seated. Her last role was in *La Voyante*, a Hollywood movie filmed in her own house in Paris at the time of her death at age 78. Earlier that same year she wrote her treatise on acting, *L'Art du Theatre*.

Mary McLeod Bethune

In her sixties, civil rights reformer Mary McLeod Bethune (1875 – 1955) created the National Council of Negro Women (NCNW)—formed by uniting the major national African-American women's associations. She continued to direct the NCNW until the age of 74.

Pearl Buck

Pearl Buck (1892 – 1973), the noted writer and author of *The Good Earth* (1931)—which led to her Nobel Prize in 1938—later turned to writing about the American scene and issues of family life. At the age of 75 she wrote the moving children's story "Matthew, Mark, Luke, and John."

Agnes Chase

Agnes Chase was a botanist who contributed significantly to advancing the knowledge of grasses. At the age of 81 (1950), she published the revised edition of *Grasses of the United States*. At the age of 93, with Cornelia D. Niles, she published *Index of Grass Species*.

Dame Agatha Christie

At the age of 84, Dame Agatha Christie (1890 – 1976) oversaw the 1974 revision of the movie *Murder on the Orient Express* (based on her novel of the same name). She wrote until she died at age 86. Her books have sold more than 100 million copies.

Ella Deloria

Ella Deloria (1889 – 1971), a Yankton Sioux Native American linguist and author, was a true keeper of her culture. She translated thousands of pages of ethnographic texts written in the Sioux language and compiled a Lakota (a dialect of Sioux) grammar and dictionary. At the age of 73, in conjunction with the University of South Dakota's Institute for Indian Studies, she received a large National Science Foundation grant to compile a Sioux dictionary. She continued working on her dictionary, publishing articles, and lecturing until shortly before her death at age 82. Her activities played a significant role in ensuring the survival and continued strength of the Sioux.

Marjory Stoneman Douglas

Marjory Stoneman Douglas (1890 – 1998) was described in *Time* upon her death at 108 as the "ever vigilant empress of the Florida Everglades." Her crusade to preserve this treasured water wilderness spanned half a century. She had written the classic book *The Everglades: River of Grass* in 1947 (at age 57). In 1970 (at age 80), she founded the Friends of the Everglades—also known as "Marjory's Army." She had been interviewed earlier by *Time* when she was 93, reflecting on her environmental work with the following comment: "It's women's business to be interested in the environment. It's an extended form of housekeeping."

Mary Baker Eddy

Mary Baker Eddy (1812 – 1910), founder of the Christian Science Church, founded *The Christian Science Monitor* at the age of 87.

Tilly Edinger

Tilly Edinger, vertebrate paleontologist, was named president of the Society of Vertebrate Paleontology when she was 66. She is considered to have virtually established the field of paleoneurology (the study of fossil brains).

Dame Millicent Fawcett

Dame Millicent Fawcett, the English suffrage and educational reformer, was president of the National Women's Suffrage Society for 20 years—until age 72. At age 73, she wrote *The Women's Victory – and After*.

Anna Freud

Anna Freud (1985 – 1982), pioneer of child psychoanalysis and the youngest daughter of Sigmund Freud, wrote *Beyond the Best Interests of the Child* at age 78 (1973).

Betty Friedan

Betty Friedan (1921 – 2006), the American feminist author, published *The Feminine Mystique* at age 42—which explored the identity and causes of the frustrations of modern women in traditional roles. At age 72, she published *The Fountain of Age*—which explodes misconceptions about aging. At age 76, she published *Beyond Gender: The New Politics of Work and Family*—in which she contends that the time has come for women and men to move beyond identity politics and gender-based, single-issue political activism.

Martha Graham

Dancer and dance choreographer Martha Graham reigned for more than half a century as the indisputable high priestess of modern dance. She continued to dance until she was 75, and choreographed her last work (*Maple Leaf Rag*) in 1990 at the age of 96.

Elizabeth Sanderson Haldane

Elizabeth Sanderson Haldane (1862 – 1937), the Scottish social-welfare worker and author, was the first woman to be a justice of the peace in Scotland—appointed in 1920 at the age of 58. The year she died, at age 75, she published *From One Century to Another*—a book of her reminiscences.

Ethel Browne Harvey

Cell biologist and embryologist Ethel Browne Harvey made significant contributions to the study of marine biology. Her work *The American Arbacia and Other Sea Urchins*, published when she was 71 in 1956, advanced our understanding of the biology of how cells divide and develop.

Lillian Hellman

The gifted playwright Lillian Hellman (1907 – 1984) came before the House Un-American Activities Committee in 1952 during the McCarthy era and expressed the celebrated phrase "I can't cut my conscience to fit this year's fashions." She subsequently described this low period in American politics in her memoir *Scoundrel Time*, written when she was 69 in 1976.

Julia Ward Howe

Julia Ward Howe (1819 – 1910) was an American reformer, author, and lecturer best known for writing the "Battle Hymn of the Republic" in 1862 (when she was 43). The hymn was published in *The Atlantic Monthly*. She edited *Women's Journal* from 1870 to 1890 (age 71). At age 89 (in 1908), she became the first woman elected to the American Academy of Arts and Letters.

Fusae Ichikawa

Fusae Ichikawa (1893 – 1981), the Japanese feminist and politician, formed the Women's Suffrage League in Japan in 1924, Following World War II, she became head of the new Japan Women's League—which in 1945 secured the right for women to vote. From 1952 to 1971 (when she was age 78), she served in the National Diet of Japan—fighting for wider women's rights and battling corruption. After defeat in 1971, she triumphantly returned to parliament in 1975 (at age 82)—where she continued to serve until age 87.

Helen Keller

In 1955, at the age of 75, Helen Keller—blind, deaf, and mute since she was nineteen months old—published *Teacher*, in honor of her miracle-worker teacher Annie Sullivan.

Selma Lagerlof

Selma Lagerlof (1858 – 1940), the Swedish novelist whose storytelling was rooted in legend, became the first woman to receive the Nobel Prize in Literature (in 1909 at age 51). Her works drew heavily on the legends and traditions of her native Varmland in west central Sweden. She wrote her trilogy *The Rings of the Lowenskolds* between the age of 67 and 70.

Golda Meir

Golda Meir (1898 – 1978) was Prime Minister of Israel from 1969 to 1974 (between age 70 and 76).

Sister Gertrude Morgan

At the age of 39, Sister Gertrude Morgan (1900 – 1980)—in partnership with two other women—started an orphanage (Gentilly) in New Orleans. She devoted herself to this work, which she saw as her mission in life. The orphanage grew, thrived, and made a tremendous contribution to the community thanks to Sister Gertrude's efforts. In 1965, however (when Sister Gertrude was 65), tragedy struck: Hurricane Betsy swept through New Orleans, destroying the orphanage.

Confronted with a devastating void in her life, Sister Gertrude began to do more of the painting she had begun when she was 56. In her seventies, her art reached maturity—and museums across the country began to exhibit it in recognition of her prodigious talent. Her work was included in the 1980 exhibit of the Corcoran Museum of Art on "Black Folk Art in America."

Toni Morrison

Toni Morrison (b. 1931) won the Pulitzer Prize at the age of 56 for her book *Beloved* in 1987. The story follows a group of slaves, from before to after the Civil War, as they struggle to survive. Morrison's writing is rich in how she describes the experience of rural African-Americans. In 1993, at age 62, she published *Paradise*—which became an Oprah Book Club selection.

Anais Nin

Anais Nin (1903 – 1977) emerged as a central figure in the new feminism of the 1970s. Her seven Journals, written from age 63 to the time of her death at age 74, provided a passionate and candid account of her voyage of self-discovery. Many women were influenced by Nin's intense autobiographical works in their own inner quests and autobiographical expression, through writing, art, and photography.

Katherine Anne Porter

Katherine Anne Porter (Anne Maria Veronica Callista Russell, 1890 – 1980) was an American writer and the author of *Ship of Fools* (1962, at age 72). She published her *Collected Short Stories* in 1965 (at age 75), which was awarded a Pulitzer Prize.

Jeannette Rankin

Jeannette Rankin (1880 – 1973) was the first female member of the U.S. Congress, serving two terms: 1917 to 1919 (age 37 to 39) and 1941 to 1943 (age 61 to 63). In 1968, at the age of 87, she led 5,000 women (calling themselves the "Jeannette Rankin Brigade") to the foot of Capitol Hill in Washington, D.C., to protest the war in Vietnam.

Eleanor Roosevelt

Eleanor Roosevelt (1884 – 1962), humanitarian and wife of President Franklin Delano Roosevelt, was chairman of the UN Commission on Human Rights from the age of 62 to age 67. She wrote the book *On My Own* at the age of 74, and her autobiography at the age of 78 (the year she died).

Anna Howard Shaw

Anna Howard Shaw (1847 – 1919) became one of the most influential leaders of the women's suffrage movement. At the age of 33 (1880), she became the first woman ordained as a Methodist minister. At the age of 39 (1886), she graduated from medical school—but decided to devote herself to the work of women's suffrage. From her late fifties to late sixties, she served as president of the National American Woman Suffrage Association. At age 68, she published her autobiography *The Story of a Pioneer*.

Dodie Smith

Dodie Smith (1896 – 1990)—English playwright, novelist, and theater producer—wrote the classic children's book *The Hundred and One Dalmatians* at age 60 (1956). She then went on to write three autobiographies: *Look Back with Love* (at age 78), *Look Back with Mixed Feelings* (at age 82), and *Look Back with Astonishment* (at 83).

Elise Stange

Cancer-researching physician Elise Stange, during her sixties and early seventies (from the late 1930s to 1950), pioneered the organization of clinics attempting to prevent cancer (especially cervical) by early diagnosis. At the age of 73, she was awarded the prestigious Albert Lasker Award of the American Public Health Association for her "application of preventive medicine to cancer control."

Elizabeth Cady Stanton

Elizabeth Cady Stanton (1815 – 1902) was one of the leaders of the women's rights movement in the United States. In 1840, when she got married at age 25, she insisted that the word *obey* be deleted from her marriage vows. In 1848, at 33, she and 55-year-old Lucretia Mott (1793 – 1880) organized the first women's rights convention in the United States at Seneca Falls, New York—launching the women's suffrage movement.

Mott remained active in the movement until her death at age 87. In her seventies, Stanton teamed with Susan B. Anthony (1820 – 1906) and Matilda Gage (1826 – 1898) to write the monumental *History of Women Suffrage*—completed in 1887 (Stanton was 72; Anthony was 67; and Gage was 61). Elizabeth Stanton subsequently wrote her autobiography, *Eight Years and More*, in 1889 at the age of 83.

Gloria Swanson

Gloria Swanson (1897 – 1983), the glamorous American actress known particularly for her role as Norma Desmond in the 1950 film classic *Sunset Boulevard,* married six times. In 1980, at the age of 83, she wrote her autobiography *Swanson on Swanson.*

Ida Tarbell

Ida Tarbell (1857 – 1944) was an American journalist and chronicler of U.S. industry. Her *History of the Standard Oil Company* (1904), which she wrote at age 47, focused on the unfair competitive practices John D. Rockefeller used against small petroleum producers. The book made visible the new role of women as muckraking journalists. She later wrote the history *The Nationalizing of Business* in 1936 at age 79. This work became a standard reference on American economic growth after the Civil War. Her last book was her autobiography *All in the Day's Work,* written when she was 82.

Marie Tussaud

Marie Tussaud, better known as Madame Tussaud (1761 – 1850), learned the art of wax modeling from her uncle. Just prior to the French Revolution she was the art tutor to Louis XVI's sister, and was later imprisoned as a loyalist. During the Reign of Terror she was forced to make death masks from heads upon their being served by the guillotine. Later she was able to return to making wax models, her collection consisting of both heroes and rogues.

After touring Britain with her figures for 33 years, she finally set up a permanent collection of life-size wax portraits on Baker Street in London at age 74 (1835). Many of the original works of her noted contemporaries are still preserved, including Voltaire, Sir Walter Scott, and Benjamin Franklin.

Kath Walker

Kath Walker (1920 – 1993), the Australian poet and activist for Aboriginal rights, became the first Aboriginal poet to be published in English in 1964 (at age 44) with her work *We Are Going.* In 1972, she wrote a book of stories,

Stradbroke Dreamtime, in traditional Aboriginal form. Winner of many awards, including the Mary Gilmore Award and a Fulbright Scholarship, she wrote *Quandamooka: The Art of Kath Walker* in 1985 (when she was 65). She adopted the tribal name of Oodgeroo Noonuccal and directed a Center for Aboriginal Culture, for children of all races, on Stradbroke Island. She wrote *The Rainbow Serpent* in 1988, when she was 68.

Eudora Welty

The work of American short-story writer and novelist Eudora Welty (1909 – 2001) draws heavily from her experience in growing up in Mississippi. Her writings combine psychological sophistication with humor. She has received two Guggenheim fellowships, three O. Henry Awards, the Pulitzer Prize, and the National Medal for Literature. Her autobiography *One Writer's Beginnings* was published when she was 75 (1984).

✝ APPENDIX F ♟

*Ron Hofsess TLOW Presentations,
Training, and Exhibits*

♟♟♟ ♟♟♟ ♟♟♟ ♟♟♟ ✝ ♟♟♟ ♟♟♟ ♟♟♟ ♟♟♟

2010 (May) – Elmira, New York, Regional Gathering of Trust in the Lives of Older Women Groups

2010 (April) – Bath, New York, Trust in the Lives of Older Women Group Facilitator Training

2010 (April) – Newport, Rhode Island, Presentation to Association for Continuing and Higher Education

2009 (August) – Rochester, New York, Presentation at New York State Association of Area Agencies on Aging

2008 (September) – Montreal Canada, Presentation to the International Federation on Ageing 9th Global Conference: Training Facilitators

2008 (June) – Elmira, New York, Trust in the Lives of Older Women Group Facilitator Training

2007 (November) – Elmira, New York, Trust in the Lives of Older Women Group Facilitator Training

2007 (October) – United Nations, New York, 17th annual commemoration of the International Day of Older Persons, presentation of TLOW

2007 (July) – San Francisco, California, National Association of Area Agencies on Aging, attendee

2006 (May) – Copenhagen, Denmark, presentation to International Federation on Ageing 8th Global Conference, "Training Facilitators to Create and Empower Older Women Groups"

2005 (December) – Arizona, support from Senator McCain's office to offer facilitator training there

2005 (November) – Utica, New York, Trust in the Lives of Older Women Group Facilitator Training

2005 (September) – Binghamton, New York, Regional Conference on Trust in the Lives of Older Women Groups

2005 (July) – Bellevue, Washington, 30th Annual Conference, National Association of Area Agencies on Aging, Trust in the Lives of Older Women presentation and exhibit

2005 (June) – Albany, New York, "Aging Concerns Unite Us": New York State Association of Area Agencies on Aging Conference, Trust in the Lives of Older Women exhibit

2005 (April) – Bath, New York, Trust in the Lives of Older Women Group Facilitator Training

2004 (October) – Washington, D.C., Department of Health and Human Services presentation with Congressman Amo Houghton

2004 (September) – Singapore, International Federation on Ageing 7th Global Conference, presentation and exhibit

2004 (August) – Hammondsport, New York, Steuben Rural Health Network Annual Meeting, presentation of Trust in the Lives of Older Women

2004 (June) – Horseheads, New York, Trust in the Lives of Older Women Group Facilitator Training

2004 (June) – Albany, New York, NYSAAAA Conference, "Aging Concerns Unite Us," presentation of Trust in the Lives of Older Women

2003 (October) – Albany, New York, State Society for Aging Conference, presentation of TLOW and exhibit

2003 (March) – Tampa, Florida, Association for Gerontology in Higher Education Leadership Conference Exhibit

♦ Appendix G ♦♦♦

TLOW Group Assessment Survey Data

♦♦♦ ♦♦♦ ♦♦♦ ♦♦♦ ♦ ♦♦♦ ♦♦♦ ♦♦♦ ♦♦♦

In the interest of obtaining quantifiable data on the effectiveness and nature of established TLOW groups, the survey that follows was administered to three groups in upstate New York in the 2011 to 2013 time frame. Participants were asked to fill out the survey questionnaire at the start of each of their respective groups, and again a year later. An analysis of data taken from the survey of the three groups points out the following facts and conclusions.

❖ The range in age among the 36 survey participants was between 48 and 91. This would put the mean age at about 70.

❖ Widowed women were calculated at 59 percent.

❖ Of the 36 participants, 34 had children, and 58 percent of those had children who lived near them. However, the children who live near them may not provide the type of support the women state they need.

❖ Most of the participants reported having someone to talk to about medical problems, and 11 percent reported seeing a counselor in the previous year. However, despite having someone to talk to about medical problems most do not have a consistent source for talking about a range of concerns.

❖ Of the 36 participants, 9 reported a visit to the emergency room in the previous year, and 3 reported being admitted to a hospital.

❖ Of the 36 participants, 35 were taking some type of prescription medication.

81

❖ More than 50 percent of the women experienced greater isolation due to the loss of a partner.

❖ Nearly half (46 percent) of the participants were homeowners.

❖ Most off the women were able to cook and shop for themselves.

Trust In the Lives of Older Women Survey

Thank you for participating in Trust in the Lives of Older Women. We ask you to complete this survey so we can make the experience better for you and the other participants in the program. All answers will be kept anonymous. Please participate as we hope this study will lead to a better program for all.

1.)   Age:

2.)   Street on which you lived at age 12:

3.)   Town / City of Residence:

4.)   State of Residence:

5.)   Zip Code of Residence:

6.)   Married: Yes / No

7.)   Widowed? Yes / No

8.)   Have Children: Yes / No

    8a.)   If yes: How many children do you have?

    8b.)   If yes: Do your children live nearby? Yes / No

    8c.)   If yes: Are your children helpful in the home? Yes / No

9.)   Do you live in your own home? Yes / No

    9a.)   If you live in your own house: How many other people live with you?

9b.) If you live in your own home: Have you considered moving into a nursing facility or assisted living facility in the last month? Yes / No

9c.) If you live in your own home: Have you considered moving into a nursing facility or assisted living facility in the last year? Yes / No

9d.) If you live in your own home: Have you considered moving in with children or family in the last month? Yes / No

9e.) If you live in your own home: Have you considered moving in with children or family in the last year? Yes / No

9f.) If you live in your own home: How long have you lived in your current home / apartment?

10.) In the last year how many trips to the emergency room have you taken?

10a.) How many such trips resulted in admissions to the hospital?

11.) In the last month how many trips to the emergency room have you taken?

11a.) How many such trips resulted in admissions to the hospital?

12.) In the last year how many trips to see your personal physician have you taken?

13.) In the last month how many trips to see your personal physician have you taken?

14.) Currently how many different medications (both prescription and non-prescription) do you take?

14a.) Of those how many are prescription medications?

14b.) Does this number represent more or less prescription medications than the number you were taking one year ago? More / Less

15.) In the last year have you visited a counselor / psychiatrist / psychologist / clergy member for personal counseling? Yes / No

16.) In the last month have you visited a counselor / psychiatrist / psychologist / clergy member for personal counseling? Yes / No

17.) Do you currently receive in-home services for assistance with daily living tasks? Yes / No

18.) Do you plan on beginning to receive or continuing to receive such in-home services within the next year? Yes / No

19.) Do you cook for yourself? Yes / No

20.) Do you shop for your own food? Yes / No

21.) Do you feel you have someone to talk to about your medical problems? Yes / No

    21a.) If yes : Who?

22.) Over the last year has your quality of live gotten better or worse? Better / Worse

✝ Bibliographic References ᵻᵻᵻ

AARP (2007). *Family Caregiving Valued at $350 Billion*. Retrieved from *http://www.aarp.org/aarp/presscenter/pressrelease/articles/family_caregiving.html*.

Baltes, P., and M. Baltes (1990). *Successful Aging: Perspectives from the Behavioral Sciences*. New York: Cambridge University Press.

Berkman, L. F., et al. (2000). "From Social Integration to Health: Durkheim in the New Millennium." *Social Science & Medicine* 51:843–57.

Bossuyt, N., et al. (2003). "Socio-economic Inequalities in Health Expectancy in Belgium." *Public Health* 118(1).

Brooks, D. (2006). "All You Need Is Love – and Very High Levels of Oxytocin." *International Herald Tribune*.

Butler, R. (1969). "Age-ism: Another Form of Bigotry." *Gerontology* 9(4):243–45.

Canetto, S. S., and D. Lester (1998). "Gender, Culture, and Suicidal Behavior." *Transcultural Psychiatry* 35:163–91.

Canetto, S. S., et al. (1995). "Typical and Optimal Aging in Women and Men: Is There a Double Standard?" *International Journal of Aging and Human Development* 40:1–21.

Cassel, J. C. (1976). "The Contribution of the Social Environment to Host Resistance." *American Journal of Epidemiology* 104:107–23.

Christakis, N. A., and J. H. Fowler (2009). *Connected: The Surprising Power of Other Social Networks and How They Shape Our Lives*. New York: Little, Brown & Co.

Cobb, S. (1976). "Social Support As a Moderator of Life Stress." *Psychosomatic Medicine* 38:300–14.

Cohen, S., and T. A. Wells (1985). "Stress, Social Support, and the Buffering Hypothesis." *Psychological Bulletin* 98:310–57.

Coward, R. T., and J.A. Krout (1998). *Aging in Rural Settings: Life Circumstances and Distinctive Features*. New York: Springer.

Crawford, M., and R. K. Unger (2000). *Women and Gender: A Feminist Psychology* (3rd ed.). New York: McGraw-Hill.

French, M. (1992). *The War Against Women*. New York: Ballantine.

Gannon, L. R. (1999). *Women and Aging: Transcending the Myths*. New York: Routledge.

Garner, J. D., and S. O. Mercer (eds.) (2001). *Women as They Age* (2nd ed.). Binghamton, NY: The Haworth Press.

Gibb, J. R. (1978). *Trust: A New View of Personal and Organizational Development*. Los Angeles: The Guild of Tutors Press.

Gilligan, C. (1993). *In a Different Voice: Psychological Theory and Women's Development*. Cambridge: Harvard University Press.

Glasser, W. (1998). *Choice Theory: A New Psychology of Personal Freedom*. New York: HarperCollins.

Global Action on Aging (2007, June 27). "Iraq: Sick, Elderly Iraqis Living on the Edge." Retrieved from *http://www.globalaging.org.html*.

Ibid. (2008, September 17). "Single Women Are in Peril of Achieving a Financially Secure Retirement." Retrieved from *http://www.globalaging.org.html*.

Ibid. (2008, September 18). "Women, Baby Boomers Swell Ranks of Vancouver's Homeless." Retrieved from *http://www.globalaging.org.html*.

Ibid. (2008, October 17). "Time to Tackle Poverty Amongst the Most Vulnerable Groups, Including Older People and Older Women in Particular." Retrieved from *http://www.globalaging.org. html*.

Ibid. (2008, October 22). "The Maltreatment of Older People in Spain Has Increased 47% in the Last Five Years." Retrieved from *http://www.globalaging.org.html*.

Ibid. (2008, October 27). "Poland Retirement Worries Grow." Retrieved from *http://www.globalaging.org.html*.

Ibid. (2008, October 31). "United Kingdom: One Million Pensioners Living on Their Own." Retrieved from *http://www.globalaging.org.html*.

Ibid. (2008, November 10). "Defining the Grandma Effect." Retrieved from *http://www.globalaging.org.html*.

Ibid. (2008, November 10). "North Carolina Slices Funds for Elderly." Retrieved from *http://www.globalaging.org.html*.

Ibid. (2008, November 17). "NGO Advocates for Older Women Moving Forward." Retrieved from *http://www.globalaging.org.html*.

Ibid. (2008, November 24). "Tanzania: No Country for Older Women." Retrieved from *http://www.globalaging.org.html*.

Ibid. (2009, June 24). "Social Support, Networking, and Aging." Retrieved from *http://www.globalaging.org.html*.

Gottfredson, L. S. (1981). "Circumscription and Compromise: A Developmental Theory of Occupational Aspirations." *Journal of Counseling Psychology* 28(6):545–79.

Gottfredson, L. S. (1996). "Gottfredson's Theory of Circumscription and Compromise," in D. Brown and L. Brooks (eds.), *Career Choice and Development* (3rd ed.). San Francisco: Jossey-Bass, pp. 179–232.

Gurlanik, J., et al. (1991). "Morbidity and Disability in Older Persons in the Years Prior to Death." *American Journal of Public Health* 8(4):443–47.

Hess, B. H. (1990). "The Demographic Parameters of Gender and Aging." *Generations* 14:12–16.

Hofsess, R. (1980). "Correlating Interpersonal Trust Scores with Life Satisfaction Scores of Older Adults." Doctoral dissertation, North Carolina State University.

Hoskins, I. (1991). "U.N. Examines Vulnerability Among Older Women." *Ageing International* 53.

Jacobs, R. (1993). "Expanding Social Roles for Older Women," in J. Allen and A. J. Pifer (eds.), *Women on the Front Lines*. Washington D.C.: Urban Institute Press.

Manor, O., et al. (2004). "Educational Differentials in Mortality from Cardiovascular Disease Among Men and Women: The Israel Longitudinal Mortality Study." *Annals of Epidemiology* 14(7):453–60.

McMillan, D. W., and D. M. Chavis (1986). "Sense of Community: A Definition of Theory." *Journal of Community Psychology* 14:6–23.

Mollard, W. (1995). "Aging and the Meaning of Life." *Expression* 8(4). Available online at *http://64.26.138.100/naca_main.html.*

Parker-Pope, T. (2009, April 20). "What Are Friends For? A Longer Life." *The New York Times.*

Putnam, R. D. (2001). *Bowling Alone*. New York: Touchstone.

Sadik, N. (1997). "What Was Said." *Ageing International* Winter/Spring:5–7.

Sarason, B. R., G. R. Pierce, and I. B. Sarason (1990). "Social Support: The Sense of Acceptance and the Role of Relationships," in B. R. Sarason, I. B. Sarason, and G. R. Pierce (eds.), *Social Support: An Interactional View*. New York: Wiley, pp. 95–128.

Shearer, N., and J. Fleury (2006). "Social Support Promoting Health in Older Women." *Journal of Women & Aging* 18(4).

Shenk, D., and W. A. Achenbaum (eds.) (1994). *Changing Perceptions of Aging and the Aged*. New York: Springer.

Taylor, S. E. et al. (2000). "Biobehavioral Responses to Stress in Females: Tend-and-Befriend, Not Fight-or-Flight." *Psychological Review* 107(3):411–29.

Torrez, D. J. (1997). "The Health of Older Women: A Diverse Experience," in J. M. Coyle (ed.), *Handbook on Women and Aging*. Westport, CT: Greenwood Press, pp. 131–48.

United Nations (1995a). *The World's Women 1995: Trends and Statistics*. New York: United Nations Publications.

Ibid. (1995b). *Bulletin on Ageing* 2/3:3.

United Nations Centre for Social Development at Humanitarian Affairs (1991). *The World Population Ageing Situation*. New York: United Nations Publications.

Unger, R. K. (ed.) (2001). *Handbook of the Psychology of Women and Gender*. New York: Wiley.

Unger, R., and M. Crawford (1992). *Women and Gender*. New York: McGraw-Hill.

Wallston, B. S., et al. (1983). "Social Support and Physical Health." *Health Psychology* 2(4):367–91.

WHO (World Health Organization) (2007). *Women, Ageing and Health: A Framework for Action, Focus on Gender*.

Wong, P. (1998). "Spirituality, Meaning, and Successful Aging," in P. T. Wong and P. Fry (eds.). *The Human Quest for Meaning*. Mahwah, NJ: Lawrence Erlbaum.

Worell, J., and C. D. Goodheart (eds.) (2006). *Handbook of Girls' and Womens' Psychological Health: Gender and Well-Being Across the Life Span*. New York: Oxford University Press.

Yasuda, N., et al. (1997). "Relation of Social Network Characteristics to Five-year Mortality Among Young-Old Versus Old-Old White Women in an Urban Community." *American Journal of Epidemiology* 146(6):516–23.

ABOUT THE AUTHORS

ﬁﬂﬂ ﬁﬂﬂ ﬁﬂﬂ ﬁﬂﬂ ﬁ ﬁﬂﬂ ﬁﬂﬂ ﬁﬂﬂ ﬁﬂﬂ

Dr. Ron Hofsess has a doctorate degree in Adult Education, with a focus in Gerontology, from North Carolina State University; a master's degree in Counseling; and a bachelor's degree in Sociology from Eastern Michigan University. Ron has been studying ways to create trust communities for more than 40 years and has been teaching graduate courses in Trust Communities at Elmira College in Elmira, New York, since 1986.

In 1993, he created the Trust in the Lives of Older Women (TLOW) groups model. Ron has studied with George Maddaux of Duke University and has done collaborative training with the late Maggie Kuhn, founder of the Gray Panthers.

Ron has presented and exhibited the TLOW model locally, regionally, nationally, and internationally with such organizations as the New York State Society on Aging, the International Federation on Ageing (in Singapore, Copenhagen, and Montreal), the United Nations Committee on Mental Health, the Department of Health and Human Services, and the N4A National Area Agency on Aging.

Dr. Christy Hofsess is a licensed psychologist and the clinical training director for the Master of Science in Nutrition and Clinical Health Psychology program at Bastyr University in Kenmore, Washington. She is also co-founder of Interconnections Counseling & Consulting, LLC, and maintains a private practice in Seattle, Washington.